An Ambassador Classic

A Pathway
of Roses

D0347785

FRANK BOREHAM

AMBASSADOR

A Pathway of Roses
First published 1940

This edition published by
Ambassador Productions Ltd
Providence House
16 Hillview Avenue
Belfast, BT5 6JR

ISBN 1 898787 10 7

INTRODUCTION

I'LL never forget the day I crossed the bridge over the Silverstream and entered the town of Mosgeil in New Zealand. My mind was immediately flooded with things that I had read of the young Pastor who first began to preach the Everlasting Word, there, in 1895. A young Pastor, though, with a difference.

Frank Boreham had a gift which quite literally touched millions. He was a born writer. From what he called "The luggage of life", he was to draw spiritual lessons and to put them in such a simple yet enthralling way, they captivated millions of hearts.

In my university days I remember coming up University Road in Belfast from Mr. Jones' second hand book shop with a heavy box full of Boreham's books which I had just purchased. Exhausted, I leant against the railings of a closed and fastly depreciating church building called The Crescent Presbyterian Church. I remember wondering what my fellow students in the philosophy department of Queen's University would think of my passion for the gentle, Christ-exalting, homespun philosophy of F.W. Boreham. They would have laughed, but, as a former lamplighter in our city, Tom Pinkerton, once told me, "Others laughed at me for my love of Boreham's books but it didn't worry me; those books got me through."

In a day of fast-lane living this book will take you to a world we will never see. Here you will walk through scenes of Victorian

England where D.L. Moody, F.B. Meyer, C.H. Spurgeon, Joseph Parker, A.T. Pierson, Richard Weaver, Henry Moorhouse, Duncan Matheson, and Brownlow North belonged. The young Boreham sat at their feet and was moulded by their teaching.

We move with the young student to his many interviews with James Hudson Taylor for work in China with the China Inland Mission. With great disappointment Boreham was turned down for missionary work because of health reasons, but, soon, the guidance of God led to New Zealand.

What a story unfolds! What rugged, lovable people those first pioneers were amongst whom the young Boreham served. We meet the ebullient Gavin and the tight-fisted Tammas and the delightful reconciliation that was effected between them. What about Seth Draper who loved Elsie Hammond but was too shy to tell her? Dr. Boreham saw the problem and a more touching story of love and romance you won't find.

The autobiography moves through Boreham's Pastorates in Mosgeil, near Dunedin, to Hobart in Tasmania and on to Armdale in Melbourne. It tells the story of how he became a columnist, a major newspaper leader writer, and, arguably, the most popular Christian essayist in the English speaking world of his day.

So many lives were touched by Boreham's writings that when, eventually, he was invited to tour the world as a speaker, few were the churches where his name was announced that were not filled to capacity to hear the man who had first touched their hearts with his writing.

F.W. Boreham was awarded the O.B.E. in the Birthday Honours of Her Majesty, Queen Elizabeth II in 1954. He wrote to a friend in reply to one letter among the avalanche of congratulations; "I am glad that the honour has given pleasure to so many. I appreciate it for its own sake, and especially for the sake of the citation, 'In recognition of distinguished services to religion and literature as preacher and essayist.' It seems to show that I have kept first things first - always a matter of concern to me."

The balance of Boreham's lovely Christian life flows from this book, which was, above all his forty-six books, his best seller and written at a stage of his life when he had considered that, as an author, he was finished. Read these enthralling lines, enjoy their sweetening influence, and follow the signposts they give which point to the Saviour.

Personally, above all the Christian books I have read, this autobiography influenced me more than any other to enter the Christian ministry. Maybe it will do the very same to others in the rising generation in the new century that stretches out ahead, in the will of the Lord. Often, when I stand at the door of The Crescent Church of a winter's night and shake the hand of hundreds of "eager beavers" who have come to feed on God's Word at the Bible Class I am privileged and honoured to conduct, I look across at the University Road Methodist Church, opposite, and think of the last paragraph of this unique autobiography. When you read it, you'll know my sentiment and you'll know how that sometimes I feel old Boreham, still near me, is pointing upwards.

Derick Bingham
Belfast,
January 1994

If I achieve nothing else, I shall at least have borne grateful and reverent witness to the goodness and mercy that have followed me all the days of my life, and to the sweetness and splendour of those companionships that have made a pilgrim track grow like a pathway of roses.

F.W. BOREHAM
KEW,
VICTORIA
AUSTRALIA
Easter, 1940

CONTENTS

Chapter 1

ARRIVAL

Salvoes of artillery and peals of bells echoed across Europe on the morning of my birth. Some men, situated as I was, would have taken it for granted that those thunderous reverberations and melodious carillons had been specially organized in their honour. Incredible as it must seem, however, I was in those days so extremely modest that no such thought occurred to me. I discovered afterwards—long afterwards—that my advent synchronized exactly with the dramatic termination of the Franco-Prussian War. On Friday, March 3, 1871, an hour before my arrival, the Prussian troops that had held Paris in a cruel strangle-hold commenced the evacuation of the capital.

But these events, momentous and exciting as they undoubtedly were, did not seriously disturb either my mother or me. We were too much occupied with each other. She was only a girl and I was her first baby— the first of ten. She and I were thus navigating strange seas, and exploring new worlds, together. *She* was experimenting among the novelties and mysteries of Married Life: *I* was sampling the novelties and mysteries of Life itself. As she pressed me softly to her breast, *her* soul was thrilling with the tremulous ecstasy and tearful excitement of young motherhood: *I* was staring in babyish amazement at the incomprehensible wonders of the complicated scheme of things into which I had unconsciously plunged.

If, however, she was only a girl, she was a remarkably pretty girl. Hanging in my bedroom at this moment, in such a position that my eyes rest upon it as soon as they open in the morning, is a portrait of her, taken in the days of her courtship. I am not surprised that my father capitulated to her charms: she was always my own ideal of all that a lovely woman should be. As a small boy, I one day lost her. We had set out together: she had missed some little thing and sent me back for it. In attempting to overtake her, I had taken a road other than the one by which she had gone. In my distress, I appealed to every person I met. It was of no use asking if they had seen my mother: how should they know my mother? So I made my first venture in the art of personal description.

'Have you', I inquired, 'met a tall lady with a very pretty face?'

One of these people must have turned informer. For, to my surprise, I afterwards heard my innocent question repeated at table. And, although any allusion to the episode covered my mother with embarrassment, I could see that the compliment was sweeter to her than any polished gallantry could possibly have been.

Crinolines had just gone out of fashion. In common with other ladies of that mid-Victorian period, my mother, in those days, affected an enormous bustle or dress-improver and was heavily swathed in several layers of petticoat. Her long and ample dress, a fearful and wonderful thing of countless pleats and flounces, somewhere among its intricate folds contained a capacious pocket so mysteriously secreted that nobody but its wearer could ever locate it. When I think of the simple but sensible little frocks in which the women of to-day attire themselves, I groan inwardly at the recollection of the slavery to which my poor mother was subjected.

As, scribbling on this Australian veranda, I recall my far-off childhood on the other side of the world, the things that most readily rush to mind are things that, at first blush, seem ridiculously trivial. I remember, as clearly as though I saw it only yesterday, my first circus. Mother would never allow us to miss a pantomime, a troupe of nigger minstrels, a conjuring entertainment, a panorama—that lumbering contrivance from which, a quarter of a century later, the cinema evolved—or a circus. Holding her hand, I walked up to the top of the road to see this one enter the town. The elephants; the camels; the cages of wild beasts; and the huge triumphal cars! On one, at a height that made me dizzy as I looked up, sat Britannia, attended by a bevy of beautiful princesses; on another sat a haughty conqueror, surrounded by his officers and followed by his slaves. Here in the procession rode Red Indians in full war-paint, with moccasins and bowie-knives! There were men of all kinds and colours; how could I ever forget the wonder of that epic hour?

And then there was the day on which, trembling in every limb, I rushed home from the infant school to which, as scarcely more than a toddler, I had been sent. My face white with terror, and my blood frozen in my veins, I threw myself at my mother's feet and buried my head in her lap. On arrival at school that morning,

I had been told that Mr. Farncombe, the old school-master, was dead! Would I like to see him? I was afraid and did not like to say so; at last stammered feebly a reluctant consent; and was led with half a dozen other scared and shrinking youngsters past the coffin in which our old master lay so frightfully stiff and still! Can I ever forget that weird, uncanny moment; the horrified flight from the school to the home; or the strange unearthly dreams of the night that followed?

But, most vividly of all, I recall a day on which there was some little commotion in the home. I forget what it was all about. I know that my mother, who was ill in bed, sent downstairs to know the cause of all the hubbub. As a result, I was haled before her and charged with having done something or other of which, as it happened, I was entirely innocent.

'And *did* you do it?' my mother asked, looking up from her pillows.

'No, mother!' I answered.

'Then that's the end of it,' she said to the nurse who had me in charge, 'if he says he didn't, he didn't!'

I was set at liberty, and scampered away feeling that my mother was the sweetest creature that ever breathed, and thinking what a horrid thing it would be to deceive her.

It is a trifle exasperating, on cudgelling your brains for the really imposing and momentous happenings of your childhood, to have to be content with knick-knacks such as these. They do not seem to be the crucial events of a man's experience, the pivotal points on which his career turned. Life would probably have gone on in pretty much the same way if these things had never happened. And yet the very fact that the mind insists on treasuring such trifles, letting slip many incidents of greater apparent importance, may indicate that memory has a more just standard of values than we sometimes fancy.

For, after all, the day on which I saw the circus was the day on which a world-consciousness was born within my soul. I had been told of elephants that crashed through African forests, and of camels that crossed Arabian deserts, and of tigers that haunted the jungles of Bengal. I had heard of conquering heroes, of tattooed savages, of feathered Indians and of woolly-headed slaves! But here they all were! I was too excited to reflect that it was largely a matter of dye and drapery! To me it was the world! All the continents and islands had suddenly swept into my soul. In bewildering and overpowering pageantry, they burst upon me all in a moment! And my memory treasures not the objective cause, which was trifling, but the subjective effect, which was tremendous!

And that ghostly scene at the old school! My memory clings to it as the occasion on which death and I first looked into each other's faces. And the incident in my mother's bedroom! It was the hour in which I learned the meaning of faith. My mother trusted me! She implicitly believed my word! The whole scheme of life seemed a grander, holier thing from that memorable moment.

CHAPTER 2

HOME

HEINRICH HEINE used to say that a man should be very careful in the selection of his parents. That being so, I certainly deserve to be congratulated on my choice. The thought of my father and mother—to whom, whilst they were yet in their prime, one of my earliest books was dedicated—fills me with gratitude on two grounds. I am devoutly thankful to have had *such* parents: and I am thankful to have had such parents for *so long*. When I was young, they were young enough to be my companions and confidants; and they followed me with their affectionate sympathy, kindly criticism and exaggerated appreciation until practically all my books had been written and until my last charge had been laid down. Not until my father had read aloud to my mother the original proofs of *The Passing of John Broadbanks* did they fold their hands to rest. My mother died in 1929: my father in 1932. In 1936 I paid several pilgrimages to their honoured grave.

In the old days they exhibited an extraordinary genius for making home wonderfully attractive to their boys. For, in my time, we were all boys. Later on, after the commanding influence of my seniority had, through my transference from a scholastic to a commercial career, been somewhat relaxed, a couple of girls were admitted to the charmed circle. But that was obviously an afterthought; and I regarded it as a somewhat daring innovation on the part of my next brother, to whom I had relegated my authority. In the days that marked these feminine arrivals I no longer considered myself a boy. Like my father and my grandfather, I required a couple of numerals in which to state my age; and I therefore looked upon the family with a lofty, patronizing air; and poked fun at my brother when things went awry. With that later and more complicated era I am, however, not concerned. When *I* was a boy, we were all boys; and it is of that iron age that I am now thinking.

We were all encouraged to play cricket, to swim, and to indulge in all healthy sports. In some respects our tastes differed: one was keen on this pastime; another on that. But, on one point, we were all agreed. Our lot was cast in an inland town and we thought that there could be no excitement in the world like the excitement of walking to some spot from which we could see the sea. There was a tradition among the boys of our neighbourhood that, on a clear day, the sea could be seen from Crowborough Beacon—a lofty eminence eight miles away. I never saw the sea from Crowborough Beacon and I never met anybody else who had seen it. But what—to a boy—had that to do with it? I wonder how many times I trudged those sixteen mortal miles! All the week we would lay our plans for the great expedition. The place at which we should meet; the hour at which we should start; the things that we should each of us take! And then Saturday morning came; and, full of expectancy, we set out. It always took the whole day, and we usually reached home at night too tired to sleep. We never, as I say, saw the sea; and we never heard of anybody who had seen it. Yet all the way, along those rough and dusty roads, we talked of nothing else but of the ships that we should see from Crowborough Beacon. We should see the gleaming sails of great merchantmen bringing furs from Canada, rice from India, tea from China or ivory from Ceylon; we should see the smoking funnels of the huge liners coming, heavily laden, from Australia or the Cape! We might—you never know— see some great battleship returning from a long spell in the Mediterranean or on the China station! Hour after hour, often beneath a burning sun, we boys trudged on along those interminable country roads, talking as confidently and excitedly of the ships that we should see from Crowborough Beacon as if Crowborough Beacon were but a pebble's cast from the sands and the surf. A cat has nine lives but a child's expectancy has a thousand.

This yearning to walk to within sight of the sea characterized us all; but, in other respects, we developed individual tastes. Very fortunately my own personal fancy turned to cricket. Cricket has always meant much to me. I am credited, in *Who's Who*, with never having been absent from the Melbourne Cricket Ground when a match was in progress except when my house was on fire. Since no such conflagration has yet taken place, that stern test has never been applied, and my wife is a little doubtful as to what will happen when the great day comes. But, seriously, I have devoted so much time to the game for three reasons. (1) I love it. (2) I find it the most perfect holiday.

If I go to the beach or the bush my mind runs on sermons and articles: if I go to cricket, I forget everything but runs and wickets. And (3) I have found it good to form a set of delightful friendships outside the circle in which I habitually move. I review quite impenitently the hundreds of long and leisurely days that I have spent at cricket.

Often as I played the game in the old days, and passionately as I always loved it, I never excelled upon the field. No happenings haunt the memory so vividly as the thrills, the sensations and the dramatic incidents of cricket. Had I ever done anything worth while, I could not have forgotten it; yet only one exploit recurs to me, and of that I am not particularly proud. I was playing at Speldhurst—a village near my home—for the school eleven. The last over of the day was being bowled when I suddenly covered myself with glory. We had made 143: the village boys had lost nine wickets for 118. Our fast bowler was put on; their crack batsman, who had been at the crease all through the innings, faced him; and I was in the slips. We were really not excited: we had no hope of securing the coveted wicket: and, always a little absent-minded, I was dreaming of a birthday party at which I was to spend the evening. All at once, I was conscious that my companions were dancing round me, patting my back, shaking my hand, and generally behaving as though they had taken leave of their senses. On making inquiries I learned that our fast bowler had sent down a particularly wild delivery at a furious pace; their batsman so far forgot himself as to lash at it; it flew like a flash of lightning above my head; I, mechanically and automatically, shot up a hand; and, by some extraordinary stroke of fortune, the ball stuck in it! So far as I can remember, that was my only approximation to brilliance at the game that was always so dear to me. I can therefore claim to have loved it for its own sake rather than for the sake of any renown that it has brought me!

Although they entered to the full into all such delights, however, my father and mother guarded against the danger of our focusing our attention too exclusively on fun that was far afield. The bagatelle board was opened every evening in the dining-room. Father was a busy man and worked at his books and his papers until long after the rest of us had retired; yet he took his part in every game; and, when it was his turn to use the cue, he rose with eyes sparkling and applied himself to the balls as though the only thing that mattered was that he should win the game for himself or his side.

Sunday was with us the great day of the week. No crack regiment ever made more punctilious preparation for Church Parade than we made on that morning. We marched out in procession like a small detachment of infantry. I and the brother next in seniority walked in front: the others followed two by two; our parents formed an imposing and formidable rearguard. Marching orders came from behind; and we never knew, when we filed out of the front gate, by what route the church was to be approached. Our commander-in-chief had an astonishing facility for discovering new twists and turns by which the walk to the sanctuary might be varied. We always set out, therefore, in a perfect fever of curiosity and every step of the way was made brimful of interest. The church itself was so situated that, come by what roads we might, it always broke grandly upon our view some time before we reached it.

Infected partly, I suppose, by the evident reverence and affection with which my parents regarded the beautiful church on the hill, the first sight of it invariably sent a little thrill through all my frame. I was tremendously impressed by its stately appearance, its tapering spire, its shapely pillars, its carved pulpit of white stone, its storied windows and its ornate and solemn services. We were always taught that it was an awful thing to come in late, as though we gave our time grudgingly to worship. I can recall no single occasion on which such a disaster befell us. Care was always taken that we should be in our places some minutes before the minister issued from the vestry door; and no one dreamed of stirring at the end of the service until the preacher had again retired to that seclusion.

Ours was a long pew, and, in virtue of my dignity of primogeniture, I sat at the far end, whilst the row of heads sloped downwards in an inclined plane which reached its lowest point in the baby-head that generally nestled fast asleep upon my mother's lap long before the minister had got to *thirdly*. My father sat in the seat of honour next the aisle. We had each sat next to mother in turn, and had each learned the mysteries of kneeling, standing, sitting, responding, and so on, before a later comer claimed the favourite place and pushed us farther along the pew.

I have a notion that, as boys go, I was fairly attentive and reverential. I still possess the prayer book which I used in those days, and its well-thumbed pages show that I must have followed the liturgy pretty closely. But that is as far as it went. I was no better, if no worse, than the average boy. When I appeared to be following the sermon with exemplary intentness, I was very often deeply engaged in planning the paper-chases or thinking out the cricket arrangements for the coming week. And I used to hope that not even the angels could read the thoughts that filled my amorous young mind, or see the visions that fired my wanton fancy, when a pretty girl walked demurely down the aisle and sat where I, Bible in hand, could reflect at leisure on her charms.

I felt a profound respect for the old minister, the Rev. George Jones. I still treasure a fine portrait of him, and, whenever I gaze upon those benevolent and striking features, he seems to me to be the beau-ideal of all that a minister should be. I had so often heard my parents speak of him in glowing terms of admiration, of affection and of gratitude that my boyish fancy was completely captivated. As I saw that good grey head emerge from the vestry door, and as I watched the familiar form, all gowned in cassock and stole, proceed to the beautiful white pulpit, my veneration knew no bounds. Carlyle, in his work *On Heroes* makes the Saint lead all the rest. Certainly this old minister was the first of mine. I think he must have detected my hero-worship, for, many years afterwards, when I had grown to manhood and had turned my own face wistfully towards the ministry, he—then very old and very frail—expressed a wish that some of his most cherished volumes should be transferred from his shelves to mine. And the Bible which has been my companion through all my ministry was the gift of his widow—*'in memory of the past, and with best wishes for the future'*—on my accepting the call to my old church at Mosgiel.

Among the formative influences that moulded my plastic childhood, two other figures demand some recognition. First of all, there was Aunt Rachel—my father's only sister. In the golden days of early infancy, Aunt Rachel was a dominating figure in our rapturous ecstasy of hero-worship. She was our fairy god-mother, our queen of romance and our patron saint all rolled into one. What excitement when the postman brought a letter to say that Aunt Rachel was coming! How we counted the leaden-footed days that preceded her arrival! With what boisterous glee we welcomed her when, at the long last, she appeared! With a flutter of delight we followed her from room to room, admiringly marking every movement, and eagerly pouring into her attentive ear the thrilling story of all our school-boy adventures! And when the visit drew to its close, with what bitter tears we witnessed her departure! The engine of the train that bore her from us seemed like some heartless monster, created only to make us wretched; and our walk home from the station was like a funeral march!

Now it happened that, at about that time, Aunt Rachel became powerfully affected by the visit to London of Messrs. Moody and Sankey. Eager to communicate to others the joy that had irradiated her own life, her thoughts turned first of all to her young nephews. She came on a prolonged visit, held little Bible Classes—as she called them—in the spare bedroom, and taught us the choruses that Mr. Sankey had set all London singing. We enjoyed the novelty of it all and were, in a certain sense, impressed. It at least opened our boyish eyes to the fact that there were types of religious experience beyond those with which we ourselves were so familiar.

And then there was my grandfather—my mother's father. Every morning towards eleven o'clock there was a firm step in the hall, and in he walked, tall, stately and grey. Winter and summer, as far as I can remember, he never missed. He always had something fresh to say, and each visit had a charm of its own. Of course I was usually at school when he called; but one of the pleasures of the holidays was to be at home with mother when Grandfather dropped in.

And what of my visits to Grandfather? There was always a certain indefinable element of romance in staying with him. There was the big bedroom with the high ceiling and the strange pictures on the wall; there was the basement kitchen in which Grandfather had breakfast; and there was the orchard! Oh, the wild romance of that orchard; it was a prairie and a jungle all rolled into one!

Then too, Grandfather kept a parrot that talked; and he kept rabbits; and, best of all, he kept a lovely chestnut pony. And yet a subtle spice of mystery attended my relationship to grandfather. It seemed to me that my visits to him were oddly timed. I should have preferred that those visits had always been paid in summer, during the long holidays, when I might go for rides and drives with Dobbin every day. But only one of those visits took place under such ideal conditions. The rest for some inscrutable reason were scattered over all the seasons of the year; and, to my intense disgust, I had to go to school as usual. But the real mystery attaching to those visits lay in the bewildering coincidence that, when I returned to my own home, there was invariably a new baby there. I could never make out why those babies were so manifestly terrified of me. Why were they so afraid to come when I was at home? Why did they come sneaking into the house as soon as my back was turned? I confess that my filial regard for my younger brothers was somewhat prejudiced at the very outset by their absurd timidity in this respect. But all these things only intensified the emotions with which I invariably gazed upon the person of my grandfather. A halo of wonder and romance seemed to encircle his furrowed brow.

Two things about my grandfather greatly impressed me. On most afternoons in summer there was a cricket match of some sort on the Common at Tunbridge Wells. Whenever, after school, I was sent on an errand to the town, I generally contrived to go or to return—or both—by way of the Common. And I seldom failed to discover my grandfather, seated comfortably in the sun, intently following the fortunes of the game. I thought old age, under such conditions, absolutely idealistic, and I wondered whether, in my own grandfather days, I should sometimes be free to sit in the sun and watch a cricket match!

The other impression was a still deeper one. For I

noticed that whenever I entered my grandfather's room without his being aware of my approach, he was almost invariably sitting at the table near the window, poring over the well-worn pages of his big Bible. And he evidently read, not as a duty, but as a delight. I said nothing and he said nothing. But it set me thinking. I occasionally read the Bible because I was told to do so; but to read the Bible for the sheer joy of it! This was something that passed my comprehension, and I spent a good deal of time in puzzling over the problem that it presented.

CHAPTER 3

FIRELIGHT

Our golden hour came on Sunday evening. On Sunday evening Father went to church alone, or taking with him just one of us for company. I do not know to this day whether we were most pleased to go or stay. What walks and talks those were in the evening cool of summer, by the starlight of autumn, or as we trudged through the winter snow! A boy tells his father under such conditions things that he would never dream of mentioning at any other time. What questions; what confidences; what revelations! There, surely, stands the true confessional! And we loved to gaze upon the old church at night. It seemed strange to see the stained-glass windows showing their glories to the passers-by instead of to the worshippers within. And yet, pleasant as all this was, it was costly. For it meant forsaking the circle round the fire. There Mother gathered her boys about her; read with us the collect and the lesson that were being used in church; and then held us spellbound with a chapter or two of some delightful book. It is wonderful how many books we got through on those Sunday evenings. Then, before we said good night, we turned out the gas and just sat and talked by the light of the dying embers. Most of us were sprawling on the hearth-rug, sitting on hassocks, or kneeling round the fender. It always ended with a story. And, of all the stories that I have since heard and read, none ever moved me like those stories that, in the flickering firelight, Mother told.

'Now it's time for the story, Mother!'

'The story!' she replied, in well-feigned astonishment, as though such a notion had never previously occurred to her. 'A story! And what on earth am I to tell a story about? What sort of a story is it to be?'

'Oh, tell us a story about yourself—something that happened to you when you were a girl!' To a boy, his mother's girlhood seems to belong to the age of chivalry, the age of gold, that remote and rainbow-tinted age in which all the most wonderful things happened. If he called his knowledge of arithmetic into requisition, he would discover that a very slender span of time intervened between his mother's girlhood and his own boyhood: but what boy bothers about arithmetic when sprawling on the hearth-rug at his mother's feet?

'Tell us something that happened to you when you were a girl!'

'Well, once upon a time, when I was about sixteen or seventeen, my cousin, Kitty Hedgecock, and I agreed to have a day's holiday together. She was a draper's assistant in a little village not far from Canterbury. Neither of us had ever seen Canterbury Cathedral, save at a distance, so we arranged to meet at the great main entrance at half-past ten in the morning. To me it seemed a most exciting adventure: I scarcely slept the night before: I was terribly afraid of missing the train or being late for our appointment. Long before half-past ten I was at our trysting-place, looking anxiously

for Kitty. Half-past ten arrived; but no Kitty! Eleven
o'clock; half-past eleven; still no Kitty! I learned
afterwards that poor Kitty, as disappointed as I was,
spent the day in bed with a heavy cold, but had no way
of letting me know. I was just about to turn away,
dejected and disgusted, when an elderly gentleman
approached me. He may not have been as old as,
to me, he seemed.

' "Excuse me," he said, "but, whilst I was chatting
with the friend who has just left me, I could not help
noticing that you were eagerly watching for somebody
who, evidently, has not arrived. Were you thinking
of inspecting the Cathedral?" I admitted that I was,
and explained to him the situation.

' "I wonder," he said, "if you would very kindly
allow me to show you round. I am deeply attached to
the place and happen to know something of its story."

'His manner won my confidence, and I accepted his
offer. And what an experience it was! As he conducted me from point to point, I seemed, under the
witchery of his silver tongue, to see the coming of
Augustine to Canterbury in the days when England
was very, very young; I actually beheld those quaint
and picturesque pilgrimages that Chaucer has described so vividly in his *Canterbury Tales*: I saw the
fierce Danes savagely attack the noble building, sadly
disfiguring its beauties; and, as we stood before the
gorgeous shrine of St. Thomas à Becket, the grim
tragedy was re-enacted under my very eyes. Concerning every pillar and arch, every cranny and
crevice, my eloquent guide had some thrilling tale to
tell. The medley of architecture furnished him with a

sheaf of romances. *This* was added after the sacking of the cloisters by the Danes: *this* was erected after the terrible fire of 1067: in this crypt with the vaulted roof the Huguenot refugees used to worship. And so on indefinitely. He held me spellbound for more than an hour and then led me back to the spot from which we started.

' "It would be very interesting to me," he said, as he extended his hand to bid me good-bye, "it would be very interesting to me if we might exchange cards." I had to confess that I had not brought one; in point of fact, did not even possess one.

' "Ah, well. Never mind!" he replied smilingly, setting me once more at my ease, "you must at any rate accept mine!"

'He handed it to me; I took it without glancing at it, merely thanking him very sincerely for his courtesy and attention; and then turned on my homeward way. When I found myself once more in the train, I took out the card and examined it. It simply read: *Charles Dickens*.

'And that's one reason,' Mother used to add, 'why I'm so fond of reading to you the stories of Paul Dombey and Little Nell and Tom Pinch and Pip and Oliver Twist and all the rest of them. You understand now, don't you?'

We understood.

Sometimes she told us stories, not about *herself*, but about *ourselves*. These, I fancy, were the stories that she herself loved best. I used to like to hear her tell of a thing that happened to me when I was just a baby in long clothes. It seems that, one sunny afternoon, my nurse, taking me in her arms, set out for a walk along the Southborough Road—the main road that cuts through Tunbridge Wells on its way from the coast to London. As she rested on a seat under the hedge—a seat that still stands there—I slept on her lap without dreaming of the countless journeys I was to take along that selfsame road in the course of holiday jaunts and exciting paper-chases. But, as she sat there, luxuriating in the early summer sunshine and inhaling the perfume of the primroses around her, a gipsy caravan turned the bend of the road. Trudging beside the leading vehicle was a swarthy old crone, wrinkled with age, bent nearly double, and limping on two sticks. Catching sight of the nurse with the baby, this ancient dame left the roadway and hobbled to the seat. Lifting the white veil, she looked at the baby's face, and then took its tiny hand in her black, bony one. Scrutinizing it closely for a moment, and turning it over thoughtfully, she at length remarked to the nurse, in a deep, husky, oracular voice: 'Tell his mother to put a pen in his hand and he'll never want for a living!' And away she went.

Whether this incident bears any relationship to my inordinate passion for scribbling, it is impossible to say. In my earliest schooldays I was never so happy as when those lessons came that gave me an opportunity of using a pen. I have never been able to understand how men of intelligence and good taste can satisfy themselves by dictating their letters to others, or— worse still—using a typewriter! With a pen in my hand I am lost to all the world. And here I am, scribbling still! Between this circumstance and that adventure on the Southborough Road there is possibly no real connexion at all. But, loving a pen as I have always loved it, my mother's gipsy story has taken a profound hold upon me.

And then there were those other stories—the sweetest stories of all! I have never heard anybody unfold the classic Biblical narratives with such dignity and winsomeness and charm as she could command. And when she came to the story of the Cross, she could move us all to tears. I confess that although, betwixt those days and these, I have attended many theological lectures and read ponderous theological tomes, the conception of the Cross that is always in my mind in preaching and in writing is the conception that took shape within me at the fireside in those days of long ago. Nine times out of ten, our Sunday evening closed with the singing of her favourite hymn—the hymn that exactly summed up all her teaching.

> Jesus, who lived above the sky,
> Came down to be a man and die;
> And in the Bible we may see
> How very good He used to be.

And, all through the long years of pilgrimage, I have never sung that hymn, or heard it sung, without experiencing a clutch at the heart and a moistening of the eyes as the fond recollection has swept over me of those heart-to-heart talks in the flickering firelight of the old home.

CHAPTER 4

SCHOOLDAYS

My education was of the severely plain but essentially practical type. Everything about it was designed for use rather than for ornament. It was workmanlike, if unvarnished. Save for the little preparatory establishment within a stone's throw of my home—a seminary to which I never returned after the nerve-shattering decease of the old master—I had but one school. All through my childhood, persistent rumours floated about the town to the effect that the Skinners' Company intended to found a first-class school for boys at Tunbridge Wells. My father and mother were most impatient for the crystallization of this project: they were prepared to make any sacrifice in order to give me the advantages that such a school would be able to confer: but, to their mortification, the scheme only took shape in the year that witnessed the end of my schooldays and I had to be content with seeing my younger brothers luxuriating in the privileges of which I had wistfully dreamed.

However, the Grosvenor United School, plain as it was, was an excellent school as schools went in those days. The headmaster, Mr. T. S. Thorne, put his whole heart into his work, took an intense personal interest in his pupils, and was determined, come what might, to get them on. And, beyond the shadow of a doubt, he got us on. I have often contrasted the rate of progress that we made in those days with the corresponding state of things to-day. It is possible that we were driven too hard. Perhaps it would have been better, in the long run, had a more leisurely pace been set. I cannot tell. I only know that the records conclusively prove that, in almost every subject, we reached a given point two or three years earlier than that point is attained by the young people of to-day. I myself, although by no means brilliant, passed the seventh standard examination in all subjects at the age of twelve; and, from that date until I left school a few months before my fourteenth birthday, I drew the princely salary of two shillings a week as a pupil teacher.

I think very gratefully of this old school, its master and its teachers. But I cherish in my soul an even deeper gratitude to the boy who sat beside me. Gilbert Finch, the eldest son of the Mayor of Tunbridge Wells, was my staunch friend and hated rival. The competition between us was as keen as ever existed between schoolfellows. That intense rivalry was invaluable: it spurred and tortured both of us. At the end of each month, the School Report was hung in a huge frame just inside the main entrance. The Report showed the position in his class held by each boy. Everybody knew, as a matter of course, that, in our class, Gilbert Finch would be first and that I would be second, or else that those positions would be reversed; and, save for the sporting interest of the contest, nobody cared a brass farthing in which order those two names stood. But, to our two selves, that monthly sheet spelt Paradise or

Perdition. If *he* was first and *I* was second, I was plunged into an abyss of intolerable wretchedness; I had no heart for cricket or bagatelle or anything else. Life was no longer worth the living, and, the sooner the curtain fell, the better! But if, by some freak of fate, *I* was first and *he* second, *I* was in the seventh heaven and *he* staggered out into the dark.

The extraordinary thing about this interminable duel was that it never for a moment disturbed or dislocated our fast friendship. Even in those days, we laughed about it in our calmer moments; and whenever, in later years, I have visited the Homeland, we have met and renewed that boyish merriment. If, at school, some problem proved too baffling for us, and if, in the quiet reflection of the evening, the solution broke upon him, he would come rushing down to explain it to me, looking as delighted and excited as if he had hit upon a goldmine in a corner of his garden.

He secured pride of place on the Monthly Report far more often than I did. And he richly deserved it. In extenuation of my defeat, I can only plead that I was handicapped—heavily handicapped. For I found concentration difficult, if not impossible. I was atrociously absent-minded. The least thing would send my wayward fancy wandering off on the most romantic and impossible ventures. I distinctly remember a certain Examination Day. We had been told overnight that the Inspector was coming. We were to arrive at school next morning in our best Sunday clothes, with clean collars, brightly polished

boots and fingernails destitute of any funereal suggestion.

All went well until the Inspector tested our class in
matters of geography. He asked some question about
Western Canada which sent my mind hurtling off on
eventful journeys of its own. All at once, Gilbert Finch,
giving me a dig with his elbow that almost fractured
my ribs, whispered, 'Java'. I then realized to my dismay that the Inspector was looking straight into my
face. Taking my school-fellow's violent but well-
intentioned hint, I shot up my hand and exclaimed
'Java!'

'Exactly,' the great man replied with a patronizing
smile, 'and now perhaps you will repeat the question
that I asked you!'

I was floored, for the question had completely eluded
me. His previous inquiry concerning Western Canada
had despatched my mind on a personally conducted
tour of the Rocky Mountains, and I was in the midst
of a titanic struggle with a grizzly bear at the very
moment at which he asked his further question relating
to Java.

Reviewing my boyhood, I can see that this sort of
thing happened frequently. My unimaginative teachers
obstinately insisted on asking their most ridiculous
questions concerning Latin conjugations and recurring
decimals just when I was engaged in snatching a
beautiful girl from the horns of an angry bull, or pursu-
ing, single-handed, a powerful tribe of Iroquois Indians,
or delivering a charming princess from a blazing palace,
or winning the Victoria Cross under circumstances of
unprecedented gallantry.

The headmaster, every now and again, took it into his head to have a monitor appointed. The appointment was based on the votes of the teachers, who were required to watch carefully the classes that they taught during the day and to make up their minds as to the pupil who best deserved the honour. Towards the close of a certain day I saw the teachers gathered in solemn conclave at one end of the main schoolroom.

'Have you made up your minds?' called the headmaster from his desk.

'Yes,' answered Mr. Wise, his first assistant, and, to my delight, he submitted my name.

'Oh, that would never do,' replied the headmaster, in the hearing of the entire school, 'he would spend the whole day wool-gathering!'

I have often smiled at it since; but it was like gravel in my teeth at the time. I tossed in torment all through that night and seriously considered the possibility of running away to sea. Still, in my heart of hearts, I knew, even then, that the criticism was just. It was because Gilbert Finch drudged whilst I dreamed that he so often beat me.

This selfsame school-fellow of mine rendered me one other service that has profoundly influenced my whole career. He taught me to love books. During the dinner-hour, on a day when it was too wet to play, he took me to a dingy little schoolroom, a few streets away, where, in return for the modest outlay of a penny a month, I could borrow as many tales of adventure as I could manage to devour. When I reflect on the hordes of cannibals, Red Indians, brigands, pirates and smugglers that I obtained in exchange for that first penny, I catch myself wondering whether, in the entire history of finance, one solitary copper coin was ever made to go so far. In every spare minute, from dawn until bedtime, I curled myself up in my father's capacious armchair and lost myself among the polar bears of the icy North, the boa-constrictors of the Amazon, the wolves of Siberia, the whales of the Southern Ocean, the elephants of Africa and the tigers of Bengal. I romped through Ballantyne and Marryat, Mayne Reid and Fenimore Cooper in no time. I wondered how I had contrived to fill in the dreary days of human existence before the little library was revealed to me.

And then, just as my fevered brain was becoming one confused jumble of Indian wigwams, Arab tents, Zulu kraals, Arctic snow-huts and smugglers' caves, my father took it into his head that such an unmixed diet of wild sensations was not conducive to the best intellectual development. He urged me to try a change; and, from some more sedate library that he himself patronized, he brought me the *Life of George Moore* by Samuel Smiles. I glanced through it, but could see no sign of a shipwreck or a slave-raid or a scalp-hunt anywhere. Still, I felt that, since my father provided me with the pennies that brought me such torrents of enjoyment from my own library, it was due to him that I should make an honest attempt to sample his. I read the ponderous volume from cover to cover, and, to my astonishment, it filled me with a delight of which, in anticipation, I had never dreamed. After an interval of fifty years, I have read the book again, and every incident seems wonderfully familiar. I owe to that childish experience a penchant for biography that has deepened, rather than evaporated, with the years. But this was the superstructure built upon Gilbert Finch's foundation.

During our period of service as pupil teachers, and even after we had both left school, Gilbert Finch and I attended night-classes at the Mechanics' Institute at Tunbridge Wells. Here our rivalry was renewed, with excellent results for both of us. We took every subject on the syllabus, without regard to its personal or practical value. And we passed in everything with—in my own case—one painful exception. Magnetism, electricity, light and heat—such themes presented no difficulty at all, although I blush to confess that, having no means of applying such knowledge to practical affairs, I quickly forgot all that I ever learned. But drawing! Drawing was a perfect bugbear to me. I entered for it because the classes were available and because Gilbert Finch was joining them. But it was useless. I took courses in freehand, model drawing, geometry and all the rest; but, although the lessons awoke a certain languid interest in me, and although the subjects seemed more easy than many of those that led to successful examinations, I failed deplorably every time.

The admonition afforded by this shameful collapse should have saved me from a humiliation that followed a few years later; but only wise men learn from experience. I had undertaken to lecture in a small country chapel on 'Robert Moffat'. It occurred to me that a picture of the missionary would greatly assist the effect of the lecture. But nowhere could I find one. In the biography that I had so carefully studied there

37

was a small engraving; but this was too insignificant to be of use. Then came a brain-wave! Why not draw a life-size portrait from this tiny one? I bought the parchment; set to work; and, not to put too fine a point upon it, was more than pleased with the result. On the day of the lecture I took my masterpiece to the chapel and hung it above the pulpit. I liked the look of it, and, before leaving the building, I again surveyed it with pride from the porch. Then, emerging on to the village green, I chanced to encounter a young lady in whose aesthetic and artistic taste I had implicit confidence. I explained the reason for my visit to the chapel at that unusual hour and begged her to return and inspect my handiwork. A few minutes later, we were standing side by side in the aisle, examining the sketch over the pulpit. Greatly daring, I asked her opinion.

'It should,' she observed thoughtfully, 'be a very valuable picture!'

This completely took my breath away. I had fondly hoped that, with characteristic courtesy—and charity —she might perhaps say that it would answer its purpose; but 'a very valuable picture!' I had never dreamed of so dazzling a bouquet.

'And may I ask,' I resumed, in the moment of my elation, 'why you think it so valuable?'

'Well, you see,' she replied, with a charming smile, 'you happen this evening to be lecturing on Robert Moffatt. But, in days to come, you may find yourself lecturing on other men; and *that*,' she continued, glancing at my picture, 'would fit any conceivable occasion!'

I felt that no punishment could be too severe for a young lady who could be guilty of such cold-blooded cruelty. So, later on, I married her. But that is another story.

Chapter 5

HOSPITAL

My schooldays ended abruptly. A mile or so out of the town, on the other side of a belt of thick green woods—woods that no longer exist—were the works of the High Brooms Brick Company. I heard one evening that this Company had an opening in its office for a boy. My father advised me to apply personally next morning and he himself gave me a letter of introduction to the manager. Like a bolt from the blue, this new development had pounced upon me so suddenly that it inordinately excited me. If the fate of empires had hung upon the next day's decision, I could not have been more agitated. Sleep was out of the question, and, for the first time in my life, I really prayed. I had always said my prayers—the words that I had been taught—and I had often uttered them reverently. But, at least a dozen times during that interminable night, I crept from my bed, kneeled beside it, and fervently entreated that I might be appointed to the vacant position.

Next morning, instead of going up the road towards the town and the school, I set off down the road towards the woods and the brickworks. I had no difficulty in securing the position.

'And when would you like me to start?' I inquired.

'Now!' the manager replied.

And I realized with a gasp that my schooldays were over.

It was in the course of my duties at the brickworks that I met with the accident that involved me in a long and serious illness and that left me with a limp that I shall carry to my grave.

I spent nearly six months in hospital. Of those days I have three vivid memories.

The *first* is the memory of my doctor, Dr. Christopher Vise. Like so many other doctors with whom, from time to time, I have had to do, he was the soul of gentleness and sympathy, whilst his skill had earned for him the highest reputation in the town. Twenty years later, when on a visit from New Zealand, I called on him to assure him of the permanence of my gratitude.

'Oh, my dear fellow,' he exclaimed, as I entered his surgery, 'I'm delighted to see you; but you have no idea of the horrors that you revive in my mind. It's like a nightmare to think of those old days. Our methods and appliances have improved to such an extent in the course of these twenty years that it makes one wonder how, under those conditions, any of you pulled through!'

And that is more than thirty years ago!

My *second* memory is the memory of my nurse, Teresa Taylor. She was a tall and charming Irish lady, of ample means and genuine refinement, who regarded her nursing as her mission and insisted on handing her salary back to the hospital. I can forgive any man for falling in love with a nurse, for I fell head over heels in love with her. There were, however, the gravest difficulties! To begin with, she was a devout and whole-souled Catholic whilst I was a convinced young Protestant. That was serious. And then, to make matters worse, there was the minor circumstance that I was only fourteen whilst she was over forty.

Thus it came to pass that love's young dream was shattered; but to my dying day I shall cherish the fact that, in hours of anguish and delirium, her face seemed to me like the face of an angel. Night and day, through weary weeks, she watched tirelessly beside me; no vigil too long, no trouble too great. I used to guess at what the doctors had said by closely scrutinizing her face. She would walk off with them when they left me. If she came back crooning to herself some jaunty little Irish melody, I knew that the doctors were satisfied. If she came back looking as though the weight of the world were on her shoulders, I knew that I was fighting an uphill battle; and once, when things were very dark with me, I caught the glint of tears in her eyes.

A few weeks later, when I was making headway rapidly, she would exchange meals with me. My bread and butter was cut and spread by machinery—each slice just like every other slice. Her bread was cut by hand; the slices were irregular; and the butter was in neat little pats on the side of the plate. And each little delicacy that came her way she at once brought to me. We both cried when, the long, long struggle over, we said good-bye to each other. I have never since been able to look upon a nurse without blessing her; and, whenever I have been tempted to a too vigorous criticism of Roman Catholicism, I have been confronted by the imperishable memory of Teresa Taylor. She would have thought it heaven to lay down her life for her Church—or for her patients.

And the *third* memory of those days is the memory of my mother. There came a time in which my life hung tremblingly in the balance. I was removed from the ward and placed in a small apartment by myself. I did not know that the situation was so critical; but I realized, of course, that I was desperately ill. In the middle of the night, the nurse leaned over me and asked:

'Is there anything that you would like to eat—anything that you fancy?'

I learned afterwards that, in view of their failure to coax me into taking any of the foods and drinks provided, the doctors had instructed the nurse, if I lived until midnight, to ask this question, and, if possible, to humour me.

'Is there anything you fancy?' she asked, temptingly.

'Yes,' I replied after a moment's reflection, 'I should like a rasher of bacon and a bottle of ginger beer!'

I have no recollection of that fantastic meal; but I am assured that, acting upon instructions, the nurse obtained the extraordinary viands and that I actually nibbled at the bacon and sipped the ginger beer.

Like the angel that she was, she must have sent word almost immediately to my home—there were no telephones in those days—and my father and mother must have shared her delight in feeling that things had taken a turn for the better. For, in the grey dawn of the morning, the door of my room opened and in walked, not only the nurse, but my mother! On a plate in her hand she bore a tiny chick, appetizingly cooked and dressed. She must have spent the entire interval between midnight and the moment of her appearance in preparing this delicacy for me.

I did not learn until some weeks afterwards that a secret of her own lay behind this act of my mother's. In the days of my convalescence we naturally spent most of our time with each other. One afternoon she referred to the night on which she cooked the chick, and then she opened her heart to me.

'That afternoon,' she said, 'I was terribly frightened and depressed. I scarcely knew which way to turn. Then I remembered that Prebendary H. W. Webb-Peploe was conducting special services at Holy Trinity. I made up my mind to go. The address wonderfully comforted and strengthened me. When the benediction had been pronounced, I remained in my seat until the church was empty. Then I knelt by myself and prayed for you. I told God that, if He gave you back to me, I should always regard you as His own, and I vowed that I would never rebel against any use that He wished to make of you. When I rose, I felt that an intolerable burden had been lifted from my heart. A few hours later, at midnight, we heard that you had taken a turn for the better. I was too happy to sleep, so I rose and cooked the chick!'

Poor old Mother! I shortly afterwards left her, and, after that, saw her only when I chanced to visit the town. Happily for me, I was able, during the last years of her life, to spend a good deal of time with her. She lived to be very old, and I paid two visits to the Homeland during the sunset years of her life. I was there, in

44

the old home, a few months before she passed from it. It is a very fragrant recollection now. There were incidents in that farewell visit too sacred to be set down here. As is invariably the case, our last evening in England arrived all too soon. She suggested that we should take Communion together in the dear old dining-room. At my request, my youngest brother, Archdeacon Frederick Boreham, M.A., now Vicar of Holy Trinity, Hull, presided over that solemn sacramental service, whilst, with Father and Mother, we all kneeled around the table that had so often rocked with our childish merriment.

Then, after a long and reverent silence, she rose, and, with a sweet, sad smile, whispered in my ear a question. Should she rise to share with us our early breakfast, or would I prefer to say good-bye in her bedroom? I begged her to dismiss from her mind any thought of rising. She never left her room until ten: why, on *this* morning, should she be up with the lark?

As we sat at breakfast, however, the door silently opened, and, clad in her pretty blue gown, with her cap daintily arranged, she entered and took her usual seat. She was too proud to consent to live in our memories as a bedridden old woman! A quarter of an hour later the taxi was at the gate. My father came out into the garden to cut a cluster of his choicest blooms to hand to us as the cab moved off. And, looking over his shoulder, we saw, through an arch of roses, her tall and stately form at the bay window, her daughter beside her to support her, and a strange medley of smiles and tears playing across her brave and wrinkled face.

Good-bye, dear Mother mine! I do not know how

you will appear when I see you again; but I am certain that you will not look less sweet than you looked in that early summer morning when, in your pretty blue robe and your dainty lace cap, I saw you for the last time through a riot of red, red roses.

CHAPTER 6

DAWN

I HAVE often admired the spiritual sagacity and superb statesmanship of Mr. Wesley in requiring each of the early Methodist preachers to set down in black and white the story of his soul's pilgrimage. If such an obligation were laid upon me, I should find the task fairly easy, although the path that I followed had tortuous twists and turns.

As I sat in the old church on Mount Ephraim, sometimes following the liturgy, sometimes listening to the sermon and sometimes dreaming of very different things, one problem perpetually assailed me. I cherished for the Church and all its teachings a veneration that almost amounted to awe; yet one thing puzzled me; I could see no utility in it all. I used to wonder what end was served by it. It seemed so hopelessly remote from real life and from the pleasures and pursuits of the week. I failed to detect any practical purpose in this aspect of things. I thought my father the very personification of everything that was upright, everything that was chivalrous, everything that was noble, unselfish and true; but it never occurred to me that there was any connexion between his inflexible integrity on the one hand and his attachment to the sanctuary on the other. I thought my mother the sweetest and most queenly woman of whom I had ever

47

heard or read; but I never once imagined that her affection for these sacred and awful mysteries accounted in any measure for her charm. But, after a while, a thing happened that threw a new light upon everything.

In the dear old home that sheltered my earliest infancy there still hangs a framed text. It is only a plainly printed scrap of white paper, cut from the corner of a penny sheet-almanac; and yet, if something had to go, I fancy that the finest pictures in the house would be sacrificed to save it. It reads like this:

HITHERTO

HATH

THE LORD

HELPED US

It occupies a place of honour in the room that was my mother's bedroom. It has been there for more than fifty years, but I remember, as though it were but yesterday, the day when it appeared there for the first time. We boys had a dim consciousness that things were going hardly with Father and Mother. *He* looked anxious and worried; *her* eyes were often red and swollen; both were unusually silent. Then one day the newly framed text made its appearance on the bedroom wall. We boys were only small, but it struck us as strange that this unpretentious scrap of white paper should have been thought worthy of such conspicuous promotion. Were there not hundreds of pretty cards lying about the home, any one of which would have made a much more tasty and beautiful adornment?

Yet, somehow, we felt that things were brighter. It was as if the weather had cleared up; the fog had lifted; drizzling rain had yielded to summer sunshine; Father and Mother were happier. One morning we mustered up courage to ask some explanation. Why had the plain little text been cut from the almanac in the kitchen and been honoured with a frame in the bedroom? But it was never in the morning, amidst the clatter and the bustle, that Mother opened her heart to us. We possessed our souls in patience until Sunday evening. It was in the flicker of the Sunday firelight that Mother told us all the secrets.

'You said the other morning, Mother, that you would tell us why you framed the paper text in the bedroom.'

'Well, I will. You know that Father and I had a crushing trouble and we feared a much heavier one. On Tuesday of last week I was feeling dreadfully worried. I do not know why I felt it so terribly just then, but I did. I had to drop my work, pick up the baby, and walk up and down the kitchen feeling that I could endure it all no longer. My burden was heavier than I could bear: it seemed to be killing me. In pacing up and down I paused for a second in front of the sheet-almanac on the wall. The only thing I saw was the text in the corner. I felt as if it had been put there specially for me. It was as if some one had spoken the words. *Hitherto hath the Lord helped us.* I was so overcome that I sat down and had a good cry; and then I began again with fresh heart and trust. When Father came home I told him all about it, and he cut out the text with his penknife, had it framed, and hung it where you now see it.'

It was here that I made my discovery. Here was the long-lost secret! Here was the connexion between religion on the one hand and real life on the other. I saw for the first time that there was a strong and subtle link between the services of the old grey church and the daily struggle in which my father and mother were so valiantly engaged. The discovery of that day took to itself all the elements of a great sensation. My eyes were opened; the whole world seemed changed. And among the big things of my little life the revelation of that memorable day stands out in bold and heroic relief.

Two events of my boyhood made a profound impression upon me. The first was the establishment of the Salvation Army. The uniforms—especially of the women—greatly intrigued me. It happened that several men whom I had met in ordinary life figured among the Army's earliest converts in the town; and I was electrified when I beheld them figuring in this new role. As, hovering on the fringe of the crowd at their open-air gatherings, I listened to the testimonies of these men, I tremendously admired their courage. Religion seemed bent upon surprising me: I had never dreamed that it might assume such a form as this. I made my way to the meetings on the Common every Sunday afternoon. And when, shortly afterwards, the Skeleton Army appeared, the whole thing seemed to throb with sensation. I several times witnessed the clash of the two armies; heard the members of the Skeleton Army drown with their ribald songs and senseless shouts the voices of the Salvationists; and more than once gazed upon scenes of actual violence. When I saw those, of both sexes, whose appeals had so affected me, bleeding from wounds inflicted by fists or sticks and stones, my whole soul was stirred within me. I realized that religion—the religion that had seemed to me unpractical—meant so much to these men and women that, for its sake, they were ready to bear any shame, endure any suffering or die any death.

The other event that stands out in my memory is the visit of Mr. Moody to Tunbridge Wells. It was announced that he would preach on the Lower Cricket Ground on a certain Sunday afternoon. As we walked home from church after the morning service, we saw the people gathering in their hundreds on the cricket ground. By the time that, having had dinner, we returned to the scene, the entire arena was black with people. We found ourselves on one extremity of the vast open space whilst the platform had been erected at the other. Was it worth staying? There was no possibility of hearing a word at that enormous distance, and only Father, with his advantage in the matter of inches, could hope to see anything. We had almost decided to elbow our way out of the crowd, and to return home, when we became conscious of a mysterious commotion. The police were clearing a space close to us and a number of workmen suddenly appeared. And then the meaning of the new movement broke upon us. The wind had suddenly changed and it would be necessary for Mr. Moody to speak from our end of the ground! The platform was re-erected close to us, and I was within a few feet of the great evangelist when, Bible in hand, he rose to address that huge assembly! To me, the astonishment of that afternoon lay in the circumstance that I could understand every word! I had somehow assumed that preachers of eminence must be very abstruse, recondite, and difficult to follow. I had hoped that, by intense concentration, I might occasionally catch the drift of the speaker's argument. But Mr. Moody took a text in which there was no word containing more than a single syllable: *The Son of Man is come to seek and to save that which was lost.* He used the simplest and most homely speech: he told stories that interested and affected me: he became sometimes impassioned and sometimes pathetic: he held my attention spellbound until the last syllable died away. I could scarcely believe my ears. It was all so different—so delightfully different—from what I had expected the utterance of a world-renowned preacher to be. My pilgrimage at this stage seemed to be punctuated with astonishments. I caught myself wondering under what guise religion would next appear to me.

Then came the accident, my long and serious illness, and the revelation to me, in the days of convalescence, of my mother's vow at Prebendary Webb-Peploe's service at Holy Trinity Church. I was naturally deeply moved and must have betrayed my feelings. My good parents mistook—as it is easy to do—an *emotional* crisis for a *spiritual* one. They felt that the time was ripe for me to become a communicant; and, with this end in view, my father conferred with the Rev. H. Webb Smith, our assistant minister, who, by this time, was relieving the Rev. George Jones of most of his active duties.

Before the accident I had been a member of Mr. Webb Smith's Saturday afternoon Bible-class. I loved it because I loved Mr. Webb Smith and appreciated his evident anxiety to be helpful to me, yet I can never recall that Bible-class without some sense of shame. Saturday was our great day. The long morning, from eight until two, was spent at cricket or in a ramble on the road. Then came a hearty dinner and a walk to the class. The class was held in a close and stuffy schoolroom. The result was inevitable. Oh, the struggle to keep awake! As soon as we settled down to the lesson an insufferable sleepiness crept over me. And, since it happened every week, I came in course of time to analyse and compare my wretched and shameful experiences. And I found that I arrived quite regularly at a point at which it seemed a physical impossibility to keep awake any longer. There seemed to be nothing for it but to yield. But I discovered, too, that if I set my teeth and made a gallant stand, a supreme effort, a final struggle just at that critical stage, the very intensity of the struggle restored to me all my wayward powers, and, like a train emerging suddenly from a tunnel, I was 'all there' once more. It seemed a horrible and ridiculous thing at the time; but the memory of it has often helped me since. When weariness has become insupportable, and I have felt most inclined to surrender, I have reflected on the old Bible-class days in England and have made a resolute stand.

To Mr. Webb Smith my father had communicated the strong desire, cherished by my mother and himself, that I should become a communicant. I knew nothing of my father's action until after it had been taken or I should have begged him to hold his hand. I shrank in horror from the step that, in the goodness of their hearts, my parents proposed. I was secretly conscious that, well-meaning as I was and anxious to do right, I had not passed through the transforming experience that would alone justify my approach to the Communion Table.

They had not, however, consulted me. The first intimation that I received of the matter was by way of a letter from Mr. Webb Smith. It is the first of two letters that he wrote me—they both lie upon my desk at this moment—and the fact that I have preserved them among my treasures for more than fifty years is sufficient evidence of the value that I set upon them. Apart from their direct influence upon my own spiritual development, they have taught me much. They showed me that a wise minister will make the post office an important adjunct to his pulpit. I should find it impossible to exaggerate the value to me of this discovery. It often falls to a minister's lot to approach people, and especially young people, on the most delicate and important subjects. Upon their decisions much of their future happiness and usefulness will depend. As a minister, I must therefore go about the business with the utmost care. Shall I seek an interview? But an interview is an embarrassing affair. I may not say exactly what I meant to say; and I force my friend into speaking immediately and without carefully weighing the issues. But see how much better I can do it with the co-operation of the post office! I sit at my desk and write exactly what I want to say. I am under no necessity to complete a sentence until I can do so to my own perfect satisfaction. I can pause to consider the exact word that I wish to employ. And if, when it is written, my letter does not please me, I can tear it up and write it all over again. I am not driven to impromptu utterance or careless phraseology. I am free of the inevitable effect upon my expression produced by the presence of another person. I am not embarrassed by the embarrassment that *he* feels on being approached on so vital a theme. I am cool, collected, leisurely and free. And the advantages that come to me in inditing the letter are shared by him in receiving it. He is alone, and, therefore, entirely himself. He is not disconcerted by the presence of an interviewer. He owes nothing to etiquette or ceremony. He has the advantage of having the case stated to him as forcefully and as well as I am able to state it. He can read at ease and in silence without the awkward feeling that, in one moment, he must make some sort of reply. If he is vexed at my intrusion into his private affairs he has time to recover from his displeasure and to reflect that I am moved only by a desire for his own welfare. If he is flattered at my attention, he has time to fling aside such superficial considerations and to face the issue on its merits. The matter sinks into his soul; becomes part of his normal life and thought; and, by the time we meet, he is prepared to talk it over without embarrassment, without personal feeling and without undue reserve. In such matters, and they are among the most important matters with which a minister is called to deal, the post office is able to render a man invaluable assistance.

But, coming back to these two letters on my desk— the letters of Mr. Webb Smith—the first is dated July 10, 1886. I have read it many times in the course of the years and it always strikes me as a model of ministerial tactfulness.

'The fact that you have determined to come to the Lord's Table proves,' the letter says, 'that you have lovingly given your heart and life to the Lord Jesus Christ. I know full well that your father would not have asked you to come to the Communion, nor would you have consented so to do, unless that great transaction had first been done. I did not truly give my heart to God until I was seventeen, although I *thought* that I did so at fourteen. I send you two little books which might have proved of incalculable use to me had I read them when I was at your age.' The letter covers six sheets, but this is the burden of the whole. I felt, as I read between the lines of this epistle, that Mr. Webb Smith perfectly understood the dilemma in which I was placed.

As a result, the course upon which my father and mother had set their hearts became increasingly repugnant to me. I felt, and felt strongly, that one thing was lacking, and that the thing lacking was the vital and essential thing. Yet, as against this, it was an agony to rebel against the wishes of my parents in a matter in which they were seeking nothing but my own eternal good. All through my long illness they had been put to so much trouble and expense, and had borne their burden with such high courage and tender consideration for me, that I could not bear to oppose my will to theirs. In such a matter, I felt, they should surely know better than I. And so, after stating my hesitation quite frankly, both to them and to Mr. Webb Smith, I feebly submitted. I

56

secretly despised myself for this decision. The day that I dreaded drew nearer and nearer. I lay in bed each night hoping and praying that something might upset the plan. When at length the day arrived, I went to the church feeling that I was committing the unpardonable sin. I was on crutches, and, to save me the awkwardness of kneeling with the others at the Communion rail, I was led to a seat in the choir stalls. After distributing the bread to all the kneeling worshippers, the minister brought it to me, and, trembling in every limb, I took it. But when he handed the cup to one after the other, he forgot all about me and I was left to my misery! Nobody else may have noticed it: no thought of his oversight may have crossed the mind of the minister himself: but upon me the effect was overpowering. I felt that Heaven had intervened: my unworthiness was exposed to everybody in the building: by a divine interposition the awful symbol of the world's redemption had been denied me. Evading my parents and everybody else, I made my way through a side door, hurried home as quickly as my crippled condition would permit, threw myself face downward on my bed and sobbed as I had never sobbed before.

Not long afterwards I went to London, and London settled everything.

Chapter 7

DAYLIGHT

I POSSESS documentary evidence to show that it was on November 28, 1887, that I went up to London to seek a situation there. I was then three months short of being seventeen. I had answered an advertisement in a newspaper: the firm had written asking me to call on November 28. It so happened that my father was unable that day to accompany me: he therefore asked a good old man—one William Warren, a friend and neighbour—to undertake the journey in his stead. I have a shrewd suspicion that Mr. Warren secretly doubted the wisdom of sending a boy of my age up to London, but he was too loyal to my parents to insinuate such a thought into my mind. He said nothing, but he did a thing that has often since struck me as being very astute and very fine. As soon as our business was finished he took me to Exeter Hall and, out of his own pocket, paid my subscription to the Y.M.C.A.

'You may sometimes be lonely of an evening,' he remarked casually, 'and want somewhere to go. You'll find everything that you want here and plenty of people to look well after you!'

He handed me the receipt for my subscription and I have it still.

The impact of London upon my boyish spirit was the greatest sensation that I have ever known. London took my breath away. It appalled me. I had never imagined such pushing, jostling multitudes. I remember standing in the heart of the world's metropolis, under the very shadow of St. Paul's, and shivering in the thick of the crowd at my own utter loneliness. Amid the hops and the clover and the orchards of my Kentish home, one could often shout to his heart's content and never a soul would hear him. Yet that was a delicious and tranquil loneliness—a loneliness that one loved and revelled in, but the loneliness of that immense and surging crowd seemed an intolerable affair.

And somehow I sensed something sinister in the atmosphere. Literature was surreptitiously slipped into my hand on the street; things were said to me by perfect strangers; and I detected on hoardings and in shop windows indications of the existence of forces that seemed banded together for my undoing.

I was dazzled—and terrified. The glamour of London enthralled me: I dreaded lest I should have to leave it and return once more to my home. And yet I caught my breath in apprehension lest the mighty monster had magnetized me only that it might destroy me. I was like some tiny moth, basking in the brilliance of the glare, yet fearful that, sooner or later, its wings would be cruelly singed in the flame.

In those first days in London there fastened upon my mind a conviction that I needed Something or Someone—a Power outside myself to preserve me from contamination and to nerve me to live my life in London to some useful purpose. And it was then— and under the influence of that intense wistfulness— that the situation dramatically changed.

Like Jacob's midnight struggle by the brook Jabbok, the transfiguring episode was marked by absolute solitude. I cannot recall any sermon or book, any minister or missionary, any church or society, that played any part in that secret and spiritual adventure. I can only believe that, at that critical juncture, Christ laid His mighty hand upon me and claimed me as His own.

In the hour of my newly found joy, my mind swung back to the nightmare of my first Communion and I thought of the part played in that affair by the Rev. H. Webb Smith. I at once wrote to him, telling him of the irradiating experience through which I had now passed. And here is his reply: it is dated May 19, 1888—nearly two years after the writing of his earlier letter.

'I cannot possibly express,' he says, 'the thankfulness and joy with which your letter filled me. I know only too well that we should not seek Christ if He did not first seek us. But I know, too, that He will keep His own; so, for every reason, I can rejoice with you— sought, found and securely to be kept. I am sure you will forgive me for saying that spiritual decline, if it do occur—and it need not—invariably begins with the neglect of secret prayer and Bible-reading. Satan will do his best to throw obstacles in your way, but to be fore-warned is to be fore-armed.

'I am overjoyed to know that you intend to spend your life in telling others of the way of salvation. To this end, too, study your Bible diligently. Bible knowledge is sadly rare, but you will find it to be of immense value, since the Bible is the one book for all Christian teachers.'

My mind, at that stage of my career, must have been as impressionable as a sensitive plate. The least thing swept me off my feet. London seemed to me a realm of romance and I was never tired of exploring it. For some months I made few friends; I often felt horribly lonely; and, on all sorts of subjects, I was desperately groping my way. One wet night, in passing down the Strand, I saw hundreds of people crowding into Exeter Hall. Moved by a sudden gust of curiosity, I followed. The adventure promised a new experience and I was specializing in novelties. The sensation of that evening was provided, not by the eloquence of the speeches, but by the personal appearance of the speakers. The chair was occupied by Sir Stevenson Arthur Blackwood, and addresses were delivered by the Revs. Newman Hall, Donald Fraser, Marcus Rainsford and Archibald G. Brown. I could imagine nothing more picturesque than those five knightly figures—tall, dignified and stately. The spectacle completely captivated me. I gazed spellbound. Whilst the great audience sang the opening hymn, my eyes roved from one handsome figure to another, bestowing upon each the silent homage of my boyish hero-worship. As an imposing envelope prepares the mind to read with special interest the letter that it contains, so that galaxy of masculine splendour threw me into a frame of mind in which I hung upon their words as though my life depended upon my apprehension of their messages. And, to this day, I can recall the general tenor of their speeches.

In those days London was convulsed by the excitements of the Irish crisis. Ever since the Phoenix Park murders, the atmosphere had been tense with fore-boding and the air was quivering with rumours. Then came the Parnell Commission with the suicide of the principal witness and the subsequent fall of the Irish leader. Whilst this drama was at its height, I took it into my head that I should like to see and hear Mr. Gladstone. I wrote to a Member of Parliament and obtained a ticket for the Strangers' Gallery. On the evening appointed, I hurried from the office to the House of Commons. Hour after hour, some tedious debate—related, if I remember rightly, to Customs duties—dragged on and on and on. I was bored to death. I heard a word or two from Sir Edward Grey and a few sentences from John Morley. But Mr. Gladstone seemed tongue-tied. Every now and again he came toddling into the House from behind the Speaker's Chair, bent nearly double and clutching his coat-tails between his ribs and his elbows. Throwing himself on the front Government bench, he heard what one or other of his Ministers had to whisper in his ear concerning the progress of the debate, and then, apparently satisfied, he toddled out again. He gave me the impression that he was lounging in an arm-chair in some adjoining ante-room, and, in making his periodical visits to the Chamber, did not deem it worth while to straighten himself up. His grey head— perhaps because of the angle from which I viewed it —seemed enormous: his form—bent as it then was— appeared diminutive, and altogether he looked a trifle grotesque. How I wished that the House would turn its attention to the Irish question, and that the Grand Old Man would stand erect, catch fire and electrify us with the torrents of his eloquence! But it seemed hopeless. I looked at my watch: I had just time to catch the last tram: was it worth waiting—and walking? I decided that the fates were against me: caught the tram: and reached home dead tired at midnight. When I opened the paper next morning, the headlines read:

TUMULT IN THE HOUSE

IRISH MEMBERS SUSPENDED

GREAT SPEECH BY MR. GLADSTONE

It all happened a few minutes after I had left the Chamber! I suppose that Mr. Gladstone was one of the very greatest of our British statesmen; but, personally, I have never forgiven him for not having spoken half an hour earlier that night.

On another evening I went to hear Richard Weaver, the evangelist. He was one of the old school—the school to which Henry Moorhouse, Duncan Matheson, Reginald Radcliffe and Brownlow North belonged. I imagine that few men now living can remember hearing Richard Weaver. He was a stockily-built old man: his day's work was really done: but, somehow, he had been induced to deliver an address at Lambeth that evening, and I, hungry for fresh experiences, jumped at the chance of hearing him.

I can see him now. His once-black hair was white as snow and he wore a little white beard. He preached on '*How wilt thou do in the swelling of Jordan?*' His treatment of the text has long since left me. But, at the time, you could have heard a pin drop. He made me feel that he was in deadly earnest. And one of his quaint mannerisms haunts my memory still. Whether it was peculiar to his old age, or whether it characterized his entire ministry, I cannot tell. But, when he had reached the close of one part of his subject and was preparing to embark upon another, instead of pausing for a few seconds, or quietly consulting his notes, he cried excitedly, 'The Lord bless you! The Lord bless you! The Lord bless you!' and repeated this fervent benediction until he had made up his mind as to how he intended to start afresh. In the course of that address he must have cried 'The Lord bless you!' a hundred times. Yet, in him, the habit did not strike you as unseemly or incongruous: it was in line with the passionate temper of the entire utterance; and it was easy to see, on glancing over his audience, that he had deeply moved the majority of his hearers.

Outstanding among the preachers to whom I listened in those days was C. H. Spurgeon. Yet honesty compels me to confess, not without shame, that Mr. Spurgeon never really appealed to me. It was, of course, my fault. I am like the visitor to the National Gallery who was overheard by the curator to remark that he could see nothing in the pictures. 'Don't you wish you could?' interposed the old man. I enjoyed every sermon that I heard Mr. Spurgeon preach: I marvelled at his power to attract the multitudes: I was thankful for his enormous influence. But he never gripped me as some other preachers did. It may be that I only heard him after the fires had begun to die down: his health was a very uncertain quantity: he invariably moved about the pulpit leaning heavily on the table, the rail or some other support. Still, the vast Tabernacle was on every occasion packed to capacity: even on Sunday mornings

I had to wait in a long queue to gain admission: and, glancing over the sea of faces, I was forced to the conclusion that Mr. Spurgeon moved most of the people much more deeply than he moved me. For sheer enjoyment and personal profit, I would have passed Mr. Spurgeon any day in order to hear Archibald Brown, W. Y. Fullerton, John McNeill or F. B. Meyer.

Dr. F. B. Meyer, of whose Saturday afternoon Bible-class at Aldersgate Street I became a member, captured my whole heart. I have often wondered how any minister would get on nowadays who attempted to run a Bible-class for young men on Saturday afternoons! But Dr. Meyer did it, and, every Saturday, some hundreds of young fellows flocked to him at Aldersgate Street. I seem to see him now as he sat on his high stool at his table below us—for the seats sloped up from him to the back of the building—pouring out to us the treasures of his deep experience. Every now and again, becoming moved or excited by his theme, he would leave the stool and, pacing to and fro with eyes sparkling and hands gesticulating, would exclaim: 'Oh, my brothers, I want you always to remember *this*!' And then he would lay down some vital principle of Christian life and service—a principle that, falling from *his* lips, was irresistible and unforgettable. Dr. Meyer was then a comparatively young man—in the early forties —but he was the father of us all; and, had we been in very deed his sons, we could scarcely have loved him more. I really think that we lived for those Saturday afternoons. We counted the hours till they came; and, when they came, they never failed to minister to us such hope and faith and courage as sent us back to our tasks with higher spirits and with braver hearts.

On emerging from Aldersgate Street one Saturday afternoon, I found myself in company with a young fellow who told me that he was going on to Mildmay to attend the Saturday tea and prayer-meeting in connexion with the China Inland Mission. When we reached the railway station, and were about to part, he suggested that I should accompany him. I was delighted to do so, and, thenceforth, took China to my heart and included the Mildmay engagement in my regular weekly programme.

CHAPTER 8

ASPIRATION

I COME of an Anglican family. My father was for many
years a sidesman of St. John's, Tunbridge Wells; all my
brothers and sisters are connected with the Church of
England; one brother is Vicar of Holy Trinity, Hull;
another—now entered into rest—was a C.M.S. missionary in India.

This has given the impression that I myself seceded
from the Church of England. Like Sarah Gamp, I
'deniges' of it: I did nothing of the sort. I love the
Church of England. I love it for its own sake: I love
it because it is the Church of my fathers: and I love it
for the sake of fast friendships that I have formed with
many of its clergy and its people.

But I myself was never an Anglican. For some reason
of which I am ignorant, my parents withdrew for some
years from the Church of England and associated themselves with Emmanuel Church on Mount Ephraim, of
which my father became a leading officer. This paren-
thesis of ecclesiastical dissent began just before I was
born and ended shortly after my migration to London.
As a matter of fact, I found myself, in a denominational
sense, very much at sea when I left home. Emmanuel
Church—the only church of which I had enjoyed any
personal experience—is an important unit in the

Countess of Huntingdon's Connexion. In its architecture, its ecclesiastical appointments and its liturgical services it conformed in all respects to the Anglican model. Indeed, I remember hearing my parents speak of people who attended the church for months without discovering that it was not organically connected with the Church of England. In actual fact, however, it is a Nonconformist church, and, as a boy, I listened to vigorous expositions of Free Church principles from men like the Rev. J. B. Figgis of Brighton, our own minister, and other stalwarts.

Having taken a room at Clapham, I explored the district in search of a church answering to this unusual type. Strangely enough, I found one; and, still more strangely, it also was named Immanuel. For reasons of his own, the Rev. C. Aubrey Price, M.A., a clergyman of outstanding individuality, commanding gifts and evangelistic fervour, had seceded from the Church of England and had established a congregation at West Brixton. Here, again, one might attend the services for months, or even for years, without discovering that they were not under the jurisdiction of the Archbishop of Canterbury.

I found the ministry of Mr. Aubrey Price particularly instructive and helpful; yet my most vivid memory of my association with this second Immanuel is concerned, not with him, but with a man of electric personality and extraordinary fascination to whom Mr. Price introduced me. This was Mr. Reader Harris, Q.C., a brilliant barrister and a born leader of men. I can see him now—his stalwart form, his knightly bearing, his finely chiselled face, his pointed black beard, his dark and

lustrous eyes. Quite recently I have discovered with
great interest that Dr. R. F. Horton of Hampstead also
fell under his spell. 'He was,' says Dr. Horton, 'a most
remarkable and inspiring man, whose character and
work have never been properly commemorated. He
had a distinguished bearing and an easy delivery,
which, added to a singular sweetness of temper and
genuine warmth of heart, made him, next to Henry
Drummond, the most attractive man I ever knew. He
was irresistible.' I certainly found him so.

Dr. Horton tells how, on one occasion, Reader Harris
attended a dance given by an intimate friend of his.
Having charmed everybody by his engaging and courtly
behaviour, he suddenly stepped into the middle of the
ball-room and, in the most winning way, told the
dancers of all that Christ had been to him. No one
was in the least upset: coming from him, it seemed so
perfectly natural. I myself never saw him at a dance;
but I remember an evening when, after a service, he
invited me to take a walk with him. In the course of
our stroll through Clapham Park, we passed a public
house. The door swung open at that moment, revealing
a number of sturdy, healthy looking men clustered
about the bar.

'We must have a chat with those fellows!' exclaimed
Reader Harris. And, suiting the action to the word,
he stepped in and, disarming all criticism and opposi-
tion with a captivating smile, told the men and the
barmaids of the perfect satisfaction that he had found
in Christ. I have never known anybody who could do
this kind of thing with such exquisite naturalness and
grace. I was only seventeen at the time, whilst he was

at the zenith of his brilliant career. The impact of his
magnetic personality upon my own represented, therefore, a singularly uplifting and enriching influence. He
taught me the inestimable possibilities of a life, lived
on a lofty spiritual plane, subject in all things to the
promptings of a divine guidance, and utterly defiant of
the bondage of ordinary conventions. He walked with
God, and, as a consequence, he had amazing power
with men: he had with me.

With all these gracious and beautiful forces being
brought' to bear upon me, my life resembled a lake
into which many rills and rivers were emptying themselves, yet which had no outlet for its ever-accumulating
waters. I began to feel that I needed some definite
avenue of service by which fittingly to express the surge
of emotion and conviction that was sweeping into my
soul. And, fortunately for me, I at that crucial moment
made the acquaintance of Mr. A. J. Leighton, of the
London City Mission, who was then in charge of a
mission-hall at White's Square, Clapham. White's
Square consisted of a nest of filthy hovels hidden away
at the back of Clapham Road. One of the countless
astonishments that confronted me in those early months
in London was the discovery that some of the most
noisome and disgusting slums were to be found within
a stone's throw of some of the most imposing thorough-
fares and under the shadow of some of the most stately
buildings. With extraordinary insight and obvious
sympathy, Mr. Leighton diagnosed my case at the first
handclasp and laid himself out to help me. He introduced me to other City missionaries, whose friendship
fortified and energized the new life that had sprung

into being within me. They took me to their mission-halls and their open-air meetings, sometimes inviting me to announce a hymn or take some minor part. The radiant experience through which I had passed in solitude seemed so wonderful that my soul literally ached for some expression, and these mission gatherings provided it.

There comes back to me as though it were yesterday, although in reality it is more than fifty years ago, a night on which Mr. Leighton took me with him to a mission-hall in Westminster. I have since tried in vain to locate it: it seemed to me to nestle right against the walls of the Houses of Parliament and of Westminster Abbey: perhaps the area has since been cleared of the vile and infamous dens that then disfigured it. However that may be, the little hall was crowded to suffocation, as such halls usually were. The people seemed glad to have somewhere to go and something to interest them. Mr. Leighton preached with powerful and persuasive fervour from the text: '*He that spared not His own Son, but delivered Him up for us all, how shall He not with Him freely give us all things?*' At the close of the address he pleaded for decisions, and two men, dishevelled and unkempt, stepped out into the aisle. No man could doubt their desperate earnestness. They were evidently longing to find their way into a deeper life. They knelt at two chairs in front of the desk. Turning to me, Mr. Leighton said, 'You go and speak with them.' I was thunderstruck. I had never in my life had any experience that could avail for my guidance at such a moment. What was I to say to two men very much older than myself? I was overawed by their deep contrition and obvious concern. In my very first attempt to lead a brother-man to the Saviour, I did my timid best and was immensely relieved when Mr. Leighton joined me. Then, of course, he took the thing out of my hands. In order that I might feel better equipped another time, I listened eagerly to every word that he addressed to them. I drank in every syllable of his prayer and listened breathlessly when, in broken accents, the two men prayed for themselves. I saw them rise, and, with shining faces, set off home to live new lives there. I do not think I closed my eyes that night: I was thrilled through and through.

One other memory rushes back upon me—a memory that has exercised a formative influence upon my life and ministry. It belongs to the late summer of 1890. Mr. Leighton told us that he and a few other City missionaries were going down to Brenchley in Kent to work for a few weeks among the hop-pickers. Would any of us care to join the party? Next morning, as soon as I reached the office at which I was employed, I applied for holiday leave, obtained it, and, that evening, handed my name to Mr. Leighton.

That was the most delightful holiday that I ever spent in England. The life of the charming old village: the rambles through the poppy-sprinkled fields and through woods that were donning their first autumn tints: the overpowering smell of the hops: the hours spent at the bins and in the oast-houses; and all the other enjoyments of those soft September days: how I revelled in them!

But the most vivid memory of all is the memory of the great white tent in which, every evening, the missionaries held their meeting. If, during the day, I inhaled a perfumed and salubrious atmosphere, I went to the other extreme at night. The hoppers of those days were rough diamonds. When the tent was crowded, as it usually was, you breathed once more the concentrated odours of Poplar, Houndsditch, White-chapel and Mile End Road. The stench was suffocating: the heat was terrific. But who cared? What meetings those were! How those hoppers sang! And how they applauded the solos that were sung to them! When asked to name their favourite hymns they sometimes demanded *Rock of Ages* or *Jesu, Lover of my soul*; sometimes they called for Salvation Army choruses; and sometimes, becoming a trifle confused, they asked for music-hall hits or for ditties made popular by the nigger minstrels.

But it all served to create an atmosphere—an atmosphere very different from the fetid atmosphere that actually enveloped them—and in that spiritual atmosphere it was easy for the missionaries to make their appeal.

The passionate fervour of those good men was an inspiration to us all. Each

... Preached as though he ne'er should preach again,
He preached as dying man to dying men.

I was a young fellow in my teens, eager, open-eyed, impressionable; and these men fastened upon my youthful mind a vivid realization of the stupendous realities of which they spoke. The appeals for personal decision—wooingly persuasive but never tediously protracted—struck me as most effective; and, in assisting with the inquirers who remained for individual treatment after the crowd had melted away, I again glimpsed the unutterable preciousness of a single human soul.

CHAPTER 9

EXPERIMENT

By this time a problem of the first magnitude began to press upon my mind. What was I going to do with life? I had come up to London with no other thought than the thought of following a commercial career. I had entered the office of the South London Tramways Company and had settled down happily to my work. During the long convalescence that followed my accident at Tunbridge Wells, I had devoted practically all my time to the study of shorthand. For some months I attended practically every public meeting held in the town—whatever its character or object—in order to acquire proficiency in reporting speakers of every kind. My dexterity in this art won for me swift promotion in London and I had no reason to be dissatisfied with the progress that I was making.

I look back with peculiar gratitude upon this commercial experience. Its value has been simply incalculable. It taught me to be methodical, to be systematic in the handling of documents, to be prompt and accurate in records and correspondence, and—still more important—to be courteous, tactful and discreet in the handling of men. Basing my judgement on my retrospect of those years, I would strongly advise every candidate for the ministry to spend a few years in a

City office, or in some other secular trade or profession, before entering college.

Nor is the time wasted even from an evangelistic point of view. A big business house is an excellent field for Christian witness. The men with whom you rub shoulders day by day will stand no nonsense: anything that savours of the sanctimonious will instantly repel them; but they are singularly susceptible to any influence that seems to them to ring true and singularly responsive to any approach that strikes them as sane and sincere. The man who cannot do a little solid work among such men will have small chance of success in the ministry.

I was most anxious to impress my companions in the office with a sense of the transfiguring forces that had been brought to bear upon my own life. In my immature and blundering way, I did my best to commend my Saviour to them. And, whilst I am devoutly grateful for the memory of all those whom I have been privileged to help in the course of my public ministry, I have always felt special pleasure in reflecting on those whom I was able to impress in my business days. I had with me in the office a boy of whom I think as one of my very first converts. His was a joyous though brief pilgrimage, for, unfortunately, he developed a malignant growth and died whilst still a youth. Then, later on, I had, as a colleague in the office, a young fellow named Cunningham Burley to whom I became specially attached. A few years after I left the office to enter College, he did the same. He afterwards married a granddaughter of C. H. Spurgeon, and, after a fruitful ministry of twenty-five years at Putney, is now doing fine work at Bournemouth. In a far too generous article which, in 1924, he contributed to the *Sword and Trowel*, Mr. Burley is good enough to say that it was from me, in those far-off days in the Tramways office, that he received his first impulse towards the Christian ministry.

One experience of those business days, causing me much concern at the time, has left an indelible impression on my mind. When I first applied for a position in the Tramways office, a junior clerk, entering into conversation with me whilst I was waiting to see the Manager, warned me that the great majority of the Company's servants worked seven days a week. A few minutes later, when the Manager offered me the position, I took the opportunity of explaining that I could only accept the appointment on the understanding that no Sunday work would be required of me. For three years this compact was honourably observed, and, by working very frequently until well into the night, I tried to atone for my absence on the Sunday.

In 1891, however, the Manager's health failed. He became morose, irritable and hard to please. On Saturday, July 25, in that year, as he left the office, he told me to be in my place on Sunday morning as on other days. I saw no reason for the command: no special work required attention: I realized that, if I once yielded, my Sunday freedom would be at an end. I therefore told him, as courteously and deferentially as possible, that, whilst anxious to obey him in every other respect, I regretted that I could not possibly attend the office on Sunday. He simply repeated his

77

command, stalked out of the office, jumped into his carriage and drove away.

On that memorable Sunday I went my usual Sunday way, but my fancy wandered off frequently to the office. The fear of losing my position did not, in itself, distress me: but I knew that, if I were dismissed, prospective employers would be told that I had been discharged for insubordination; and this, I knew from the experiences of others, would raise very serious difficulties. My mind that Sunday was constantly directed to a passage in Isaiah: *If thou turn away thy foot from the Sabbath, from doing thy pleasure on my holy day, and call the Sabbath a delight, the holy of the Lord, honourable; and shalt honour Him, not doing thine own ways, nor finding thine own pleasure, nor speaking thine own words, then shalt thou delight thyself in the Lord, and I will cause thee to ride upon the high places of the earth and feed thee with the heritage of Jacob thy father; for the mouth of the Lord hath spoken it.*

When the Manager arrived at the office on the Monday, he asked me to furnish a written explanation of my behaviour and I guardedly drafted the document, being specially careful to express my regret at having been compelled to set my own will in antagonism with his. A day or two later, we received a message from his home to the effect that he was too ill to come to the office. A day or two later still he was too ill to attend to business at his bedside. And, on October 17, he died. In due course a new Manager was appointed and it became his duty to review the files left by his predecessor. In process of time I laid before him the documents relating to my own recalcitration.

He looked up, smiled, tore the papers to tatters and committed them to the waste-paper basket. And thus a worrying incident happily closed.

On the whole, I thoroughly enjoyed my years in business and am thankful for them. Yet, in view of the profound impressions made upon me during my first few weeks in London, an irresistible conviction was all the time increasing its hold upon me—a conviction that it was the will of God that I should devote all my time and dedicate all my powers to definite Christian work. Oddly enough, I never, in the early stages, thought seriously of the ministry. The idea of entering a pulpit, if suggested to me, would have seemed ludicrous and grotesque. It had not dawned upon me that, with patient study and constant practice, I might learn to preach. My most passionate craving was to be a foreign missionary, and, failing that, to be a city missionary. Still under the fragrant influence of the Saturday afternoon gatherings at Mildmay, my heart turned wistfully to the China Inland Mission. I had many interviews with Dr. Hudson Taylor, Mr. Broomhall and others. Eventually Dr. Hudson Taylor invited me to tea with him; and, with a tenderness and tact that left no sting of disappointment, he pointed out to me the opportunities of doing effective missionary work at Home. My injury, he feared, would seriously hamper me on the foreign field.

'Pray earnestly,' he said, 'that you may be used in leading many of your friends to Christ, and then encourage them to live and work for China!'

Finding this road blocked, I resolved to seek avenues of service nearer home. Amidst torments of nervousness,

I began to testify and deliver very brief addresses at the open-air meetings and mission services at which I had previously been content with announcing an occasional hymn. This led to my being invited to give the principal address at a meeting to be held at a street corner at Clapham. If I were in London to-day, I fancy that I could locate the exact spot, although I have never visited it since. Over-awed by the weight of the responsibility devolving upon me, I resolved to commit my thoughts to paper. I still possess that manuscript. Happily, it is dated, showing that I was not yet eighteen at the time of its delivery. That first sermon of mine is based on the text: *To-day if ye will hear His voice, harden not your hearts.* Having in the course of my life, been honoured with a seat on many committees that had to do with the selection of candidates for the ministry, I have met with many crude attempts at sermon-making. But this manuscript that lies before me is easily the crudest of them all. From a theological and homiletical point of view, it has not one redeeming feature. It contains no exordium, no exegesis, no divisions, no anything. It begins with the application with which it should close: and that premature and elongated application runs right through it to the very end.

And yet, although every perusal of this faded manuscript provokes a smile, it also provokes something suspiciously resembling a tear.

For this weird sermon—which is really no sermon at all—is the immature effort of a young man in a hurry—a young man in a tremendous hurry to get to close grips with his hearers. In spite of all its crudities and absurdities, it throbs with passion. I know where I caught that fire. Having been infected, at that most plastic stage of my career, by the apostolic intensity and spiritual fervour of those good men of God into whose company I was providentially thrown, I was aflame with their evangelistic zeal. And, looking back across the years I like to think that this raw and callow youth, away at the other end of life, was in such deadly earnest. He goes the wrong way about it; but you cannot read three lines of the manuscript without feeling that he is desperately eager to persuade and capture men.

Oh, is not this a solemn matter between yourselves and God? Will you not hear His voice? Indeed, have you not already heard it? Perhaps in the hour of need, perhaps in time of trouble, perhaps in a moment of great joy, you have heard Him pleading within. But what has followed? You hardened your hearts.

And so on. The whole thing is set in this tense key. It stresses the way in which the Saviour speaks from the Cross: it emphasizes the doom that must overtake those who harden their hearts to the end: and it pleads for instant contrition and faith. The *Oh* with which it opens is repeated continually. When David Garrick heard George Whitefield preach, he said that he would give a thousand pounds to be able to say *Oh* as Whitefield said it. I have often felt similarly concerning those youthful *Ohs* of mine. An intense yearning is the dominant characteristic of this quaint manuscript; and, in my best moments, I catch myself praying that something of that early craving may endure to the end of the chapter.

Gaining confidence with experience, I addressed these out-of-door gatherings with increasing frequency; and, having been introduced to Mr. Gawin Kirkham, the Secretary of the Open Air Mission, I joined that organization. Mr. Gawin Kirkham held that open-air preaching, to be effective, should be well done and well organized. The Mission, which had offices at Charing Cross, saw to it that the meetings held in the various suburbs were properly arranged and properly equipped. The speakers were apprised by post of their appointments, and they were to recognize each other by carrying a Bible from which the red tassel of the bookmarker—the badge of membership—was distinctly visible. My own Bible—the Bible to which I have already referred in Chapter 2—is still adorned by that red bookmarker with its tell-tale tassel. Care was taken that each party consisted of two or three mature and experienced speakers—one of whom was nominated as leader—and a few young recruits. It was the duty of the older men to criticize the youngsters. Although done with perfect frankness, it was always done with the utmost kindness, and the suggestions thus offered proved of incalculable value.

As a training-ground for the ministry, open-air preaching has two outstanding advantages. To begin with, it enables the speaker to test his ability to attract and hold an audience. In a church or a mission-hall, decency demands that the people shall keep their seats until the speaker has resumed his. But, in the open air, people gather round if the speaker's personality and manner impress them, and they remain only just as long as he succeeds in interesting them. Whilst one man is speaking, the crowd will grow to hundreds; whilst his successor is holding forth, it will dwindle to a mere handful. This later orator, if he be wise, will make the phenomenon a matter of heart-searching. Why did the first man hold his crowd? And why did he himself disperse it?

And then again, open-air preaching is always available. I have often heard young aspirants to the ministry complain that they feel called to preach, but lack opportunities. Nobody invites them. Why not invite themselves? If they are divinely called to preach, why wait for any human sanction or authority? Let them preach! Go where the crowds gather! Step off the kerb, or into an open space, and call out 'I say, you people!' And then go right ahead! In the old days—sometimes by myself and sometimes with one or two companions—I often did this kind of thing in London; and, if nobody else profited by it, I certainly did. Sometimes we were moved on by the police, who maintained that we were obstructing the thoroughfare; but I never remember receiving from the crowd anything but a respectful hearing.

Chapter 10

ADVENTURE

Among the by-products of those impromptu and irresponsible gatherings under the open sky—most of which were held at Clapham Pavement and on the outskirts of Clapham Common—were two totally unexpected developments.

One evening, after I had pronounced the Benediction, a young fellow approached me.

'A number of us,' he said, 'are greatly impressed by the possibilities of these meetings; but we are surprised that you have no singing. Don't you think a few hymns would make the gatherings more appealing?'

I said that I had no doubt of it; but the trouble was that neither my colleagues nor myself possessed any talent for music.

'Well,' he replied, 'we are a band of young people who can sing, though none of us can preach. If you will allow us to form a ring around you and sing a few hymns each evening, we shall be delighted.'

It was so arranged, and the drawing power of the meetings was greatly strengthened in consequence. In contact with these charming young people, we discovered that they were connected with a company of Plymouth Brethren meeting in a neighbouring hall. At the end of the summer, finding that I had no

Church connexions that I regarded as binding, they invited me to cement the bond between myself and them by joining their fellowship. By this time I had become genuinely fond of them: I liked all that they told me about their methods of worship: and I assented cordially to their proposal. I was duly interrogated by a deputation that waited upon me and was assured that my application would be warmly approved.

In due time I was notified of my acceptance and was asked to present myself on a certain Sunday morning in order that the right hand of fellowship might be extended to me. On entering the hall, I noticed that the young people with whom I had been associated at the open-air meetings were sitting, with a number of older people, near the front. I was instructed to take a seat half-way back until my name was called. The gathering was presided over by a soldierly-looking elderly gentleman of stately bearing, snow-white hair and florid countenance.

In due time this imposing and somewhat formidable figure called my name, and, stepping forward, I mounted the platform and stood facing him. Just as I thought that he was about to extend a friendly and welcoming hand, he startled me by pointing abruptly to the lapel of my coat.

'Young man,' he demanded sternly, 'what is *that*?'

At first I was dumbfounded. I failed to apprehend the meaning of his unexpected gesture and strange question. Examining my coat more closely, however, my eye came to rest on the tiny scrap of blue ribbon which it was customary, in those days, for temperance workers to wear. Convinced that this faded badge was the object of his pointed inquiry, I pulled myself together and stammeringly replied:

'It is a piece of blue ribbon, sir,' I said. 'I wear it to show that I am pledged to avoid all intoxicating drinks and that I shall use my influence to induce others to abstain.'

'Young man,' he answered, sadly but sternly, 'it is a badge of the world. You must return to the seat from which you came. Your case will be further considered.'

I left the hall in confusion, entreating the young people with whom I had been so pleasantly associated to see that my name was immediately withdrawn. And that was the last I heard of it.

Some time afterwards—and this is the *second* of the surprising developments to which I have referred—I was told that Mr. Spurgeon had expressed interest in reports that had come to his ears concerning our open-air meeting, and had asked that, with a view to my admission to College, inquiries should be made concerning me. Whether or not this was an accurate statement of the case, I have no means of knowing. I only know that one or two gentlemen, more or less directly associated with Mr. Spurgeon, began to show an interest in me.

At the outset I saw one serious—perhaps insuperable—difficulty. Mr. Spurgeon was a Baptist: his college was a Baptist College: whilst, except that I had sometimes walked from Clapham to Newington to hear him, I had scarcely entered a Baptist church in my life. I had, however, been recently baptized. In my solitary studies I had been impressed by the fact that, in the Acts of the Apostles, the early converts confessed their faith by means of baptism. It seemed to me that, in my own pilgrimage, something was lacking at this point. Whilst I was still exercised on the matter, I found myself sitting opposite to a gentleman on the tram who was studying a book on the very subject that was causing me such anxious thought. When he rose to leave, although I had not reached my destination, I followed him.

He turned out to be the Rev. G. S. Read, a minister of a body known as the Old Baptist Union which had only been founded about ten years. These good people believed in the maintenance of all apostolic traditions—fasting, laying-on of hands, the washing of feet and, of course, baptism. He advised me to give myself to fasting and to prayer. For a few days I subsisted entirely on bread and water, earnestly seeking clear guidance. Then, on April 7, 1890, I received from him a letter—which lies before me as I write—telling me that a baptismal service, with laying-on of hands, was to be held at Stockwell on the following evening and inviting me to present myself as a candidate. I immediately communicated with my father and mother— I was only just nineteen—and, receiving their wholehearted benediction, I made my way to Stockwell that Easter Tuesday evening, having tasted no food of any kind that day. I was deeply impressed by the baptism; but, strangely enough, I was still more deeply moved by the laying-on of hands. The service was conducted by the Rev. H. A. Squire, a commanding and patriarchal figure, who founded the Old Baptist Union and was for thirty-four years its President. His searching address that night on Jeremiah vi. 16 haunts my memory still. He was surrounded by a number of assisting ministers. As, with all their hands piled upon my bowed head, Mr. Squire bade me *receive the Holy Ghost*, it did really seem to me that a gracious tide of spiritual power poured itself into my soul, and, for weeks afterwards, I lived in such ecstasy that I could scarcely believe that the earth on which I was walking was the dusty old earth to which I had always been accustomed. Nobody, on the night of my baptism, suggested that I should return to any of the sanctuaries of the Old Baptist Union and I never did. That was my first and last point of contact with these devout folk; I have occasionally seen references to them and to their work in the newspapers: and I have always cherished for them a grateful and affectionate regard.

This experience, however, did not entitle me to call myself a Baptist. But, some time afterwards, I fell in with the Rev. James Douglas, M.A., of Kenyon Baptist Church, Brixton. Mr. Douglas—one of the most saintly and scholarly men whom I have ever known—was an intimate personal friend of Mr. Spurgeon and afterwards wrote the great preacher's biography. Taking a fatherly interest in me, Mr. Douglas not only invited me to join his church, but he insisted on my visiting his home, and, later on, when I had definitely turned my face towards the ministry, he devoted to me his Thursday afternoons, sometimes sitting with me in his study and sometimes taking me for walks on Clapham Common. He always carried a Hebrew Psalter and a Greek Testament, and, seated on the open greensward or under a kindly clump of elms,

he poured into my ears striking and suggestive transla-
tions and illuminating morsels of exposition. Out of
the wealth of his long and rich experience he advised
and instructed me in relation to the work that I hoped
one day to do; and some of the most memorable and
valuable lectures in pastoral theology to which I have
ever listened were imparted to me in the course of those
Thursday walks and talks.

Under his guidance I applied to Mr. Spurgeon for
admission to the College and was accepted. Un-
happily, however, between my application and my
admission, Mr. Spurgeon himself entered into his rest.
I was once told that, before his death, he had given
instructions that my application was to be approved,
and that I might consider myself the last student whose
entrance to College had been personally determined by
the Founder. But here again, possessing no evidence, I
cannot, of course, be sure.

Up to the time of my application to Mr. Spurgeon,
I had never entered a pulpit. Like an eager fledgling,
however, I was stretching my wings and preparing for
my first flight. Nor had I long to wait. On Sunday,
May 31, 1891—I being then twenty—the Secretary of
the Park Crescent Congregational Church, Clapham,
called on me at about ten o'clock in the morning to say
that the church was without a minister, that the pulpit
supply for that particular morning had failed: would I
step into the breach? How I contrived to sustain so
vast a responsibility at such meagre notice, I cannot
imagine, especially as I find that I took for my text
the words: *He, through the Eternal Spirit, offered Himself
without spot to God.* To-day I should need weeks of

careful preparation before attempting so abstruse a theme. But perhaps my mind had been occupied with the subject during the days preceding that unexpected summons. At any rate, I struggled through the service, and, insuperable obstacles to the immediate appointment of a minister presenting themselves, I was subsequently invited to occupy the pulpit for five months. As soon as I began to preach, I began to keep a journal in which the impressions left upon my mind by each service are recorded. It is quite a good thing to do. Perusing the record of that five-months' ministry at Park Crescent, one thing is clear. Delighted as I was to have the opportunity of testing and developing my powers, I was overwhelmed by a sense of my need of training. I felt as a soldier might feel who found himself in the front line totally unarmed and unequipped. Embarrassed and humiliated by the difficulties that I confronted, and by the mistakes that I made, I felt unutterably grateful that the opportunity of a college career had been opened to me, and, galled by a consciousness of my inefficiency, I highly resolved to make the most of it.

Chapter 11

COLLEGE

Southey used to say that, however long a man's life, the first twenty years represent by far the bigger half of it. That being so, my tale is more than half told. For, in 1892, I came of age and entered College.

It was on a typical summer's day in mid-July that I walked out of the Tramways office for the last time. The vacancy created by my resignation had been advertised, and applicants for the position were instructed to present themselves personally at the office. As I marked the multitude of men who were eager to step into my shoes, my heart was in my mouth. Looking back, I smile at the absurdity of that momentary wave of apprehension. The editor of a popular magazine recently invited me to write on *The Lights and Shadows of the Ministerial Life*. It seems to me that a minister's life is *all* bright light and deep shade. If there are any dull or drab passages in it I have to confess that I have failed to discover them. If there is anything in the doctrine of reincarnation I intend to spend at least one of my future spans of existence as a novelist, working up into thrilling romances the plots that I have collected in the course of my career as a minister. Every day of his life a man who is really in touch with his people finds himself confronted by tangles of circumstance as richly suffused with sentiment, with mystery and with passion as any conditions set forth in the pages of fiction. Or—to put the matter another way—if I were a young fellow just setting out into life, and if I wanted a career that would provide the most absorbing interest, every day offering my delighted eyes some new and beautiful turn of the kaleidoscope of human romance, I should once more give myself without a moment's hesitation to the Christian ministry. For romance is simply the expression of the deepest human instincts; and one gets nearer to those palpitating instincts in the ministry than in any other walk of life. My own experience has taught me that he who is called to the Christian ministry lays his fingers on the quivering heartstrings of men's deepest emotions; and he who has once tasted the poignant raptures of the ministry would not be anything but a minister for all the gold of the Indies.

I entered College on August 9, 1892. In a way, this important step was singularly ill-timed. I could scarcely have chosen a less auspicious moment. Exactly six months earlier, I had stood with the students then in College beside Mr. Spurgeon's grave at Norwood. Exactly six months after my admission—to the very day—Principal David Gracey also passed away. The loss of both President and Principal naturally threw the entire machinery of the institution into confusion; and, for some months, it was a common experience for students, on arriving at the College, to be met with the announcement that there would be no classes that day. At the time, this seemed a disaster of the first magnitude; but, reviewing it in the perspective of the years,

I am not so sure. For it had the effect of fastening upon my mind the necessity for making up the leeway after leaving College. And, in the attempt to regain this lost ground, I later on devoted to study many hours that might otherwise have been frittered away, thus acquiring habits of systematic reading that have remained with me all through the years.

My College course was not a long one. It occupied two years and a half. Two factors contributed to its abbreviation. The *first* was the fact that, in my boyish studies as a pupil teacher, and in the night classes that followed, I had mastered most of the subjects that made up the first year's curriculum. The *second* was that, at the close of one of my open-air meetings at Clapham, a saintly and scholarly old clergyman, obviously pitying the paucity of my intellectual equipment, had kindly offered to give me lessons in Greek. I, as conscious as he was of my own deficiencies, had snatched with avidity at such a golden opportunity. And, as a result, I found myself, on entering College, able to take my place with the men who had already been there for twelve months.

Notwithstanding the somewhat brief and somewhat disturbed character of my course, however, I owe much to the College. I have often heard it said that young fellows, aflame with spiritual intensity and evangelistic passion, lose in College the ardour that drove them to its doors. I can only say that I saw no sign of any such tendency. In addition to our classwork, we had ample opportunities for intimate spiritual fellowship. The Friday prayer meeting, followed once a month by the Communion service, was a means of grace to all of us, creating an atmosphere in which it became easy for us to open our hearts to one another.

The Friday lectures, too. In my time, many—if not most—of them were delivered by Dr. A. T. Pierson, who supplied the pulpit of the Metropolitan Tabernacle during the illness, and for some time after the death, of Mr. Spurgeon. Dr. Pierson looms largely on the horizon of my College days. He was distinctly a personality. He magnetized us all. I still possess a series of cartoons which, in December, 1892, appeared in a London comic paper, caricaturing his favourite gestures, attitudes and expressions. We students missed no opportunity of hearing him. For sheer down-right oratory I regarded him as peerless. He would lecture at the Metropolitan Tabernacle on such subjects as The Impregnable Rock of Holy Scripture, holding six or seven thousand people spell-bound for nearly two hours. His Friday afternoon lectures to the students were no less masterly. I realized, as I listened to him, that his rhetorical effects were produced by the most diligent and careful preparation. He knew beforehand exactly what he was going to say and exactly how he was going to say it.

He possessed, as we all do, the defects of his virtues. In College we took the liberty of changing his initials. We spoke of him, not as Dr. A. T. Pierson, but as Dr. M. R. Pierson. The M. R. stood for Most Remarkable. Every text that he announced in the Tabernacle pulpit was the most remarkable text in the Bible: every subject on which he lectured was the most remarkable with which a man could possibly deal: and every historical reference was introduced as one of the world's most remarkable happenings. And the extraordinary thing was that, at the moment, he really believed it! To him, his immediate theme—whatever that theme might be— was absolutely incomparable. He completely forgot the glowing superlatives with which he had stressed the paramount importance of other subjects. Every tad- pole that he touched became, for the time being, an archangel. All his geese were swans. The poet that he chanced to be quoting was always a Shakespeare. The slope that he was climbing was, to him, Mount Everest. To those of us who heard him almost daily, this amiable frailty seemed a trifle grotesque; yet we were compelled to recognize that his tongue acquired a magic eloquence, and his arguments a resistless driving-power, from his sincere conviction of the unrivalled splendour of his immediate theme.

Almost simultaneously, another eminent American laid hold of London and left an indelible impression on the students of that day. In 1893, Mr. Moody, accom- panied by Mr. Sankey, held his last mission in London. The services were held in the Metropolitan Tabernacle and the students were invited to act as ushers. It was our duty to show people to their seats before the service; to study Mr. Moody's message and methods during the service; and to be on the lookout for inquirers at the close of the service.

I must have heard Mr. Moody thirty or forty times during that fortnight. I learn from his biography that it was during that mission that his health collapsed, compelling him to consult Sir Andrew Clark. I am surprised: he certainly gave no outward indication of any physical frailty. To us students he seemed like a volcano in ceaseless eruption, a miracle of tireless activity. I well remember a day on which, between the afternoon and evening services, he was enjoying a breathing-space and a cup of tea. He was told that, although it was not yet six o'clock, there were enough people waiting outside the Tabernacle to crowd it for the evening service.

'Let them in!' he exclaimed; and the doors were at once thrown open. He then made his way to the pulpit; delivered a gripping and unforgettable address to the assembled multitude; dismissed them; and, at the appointed time, was once more in the pulpit ready to grapple with a second evening congregation!

I doubt if any of the students of that day have ever shaken off, or would like to shake off, the impact upon their own plastic and impressionable minds of the rugged and commanding personality of Mr. Moody. As Dr. J. Stuart Holden said at the time, 'Moody's flaming evangelism, his zeal for souls, his transparent honesty, his loyalty to God's Word, his passion for exalting Christ; these endeared him to thousands to whom he will always stand for the best things of their Christian experience'. It is very pleasant now to reflect that, as a small boy, I fell under the magic of Mr. Moody when, on the day on which the wind so suddenly changed, he visited my own home-town; and that, later on, as a theological student, I saw him close his memorable English ministry.

At that mission, each student was allotted a little block of seats. We were carefully instructed as to the way in which we were to shepherd the people in those pews. We were to see that every one was comfortable;

that every one was supplied with a hymn-book; and
that, without undue button-holing, those who needed
individual counsel could readily find it. I like to
remember that, among those who attended the afternoon meetings, and who occupied a front seat in the
section apportioned to me, was a stately young lady
in black who listened to Mr. Moody with marked
reverence and the very closest attention. We knew her
then as Princess May, the daughter of the Duke and
Duchess of Teck. But I have lived to see her become,
in turn, the Duchess of York, the Princess of Wales, the
Queen of England, and the Venerable Queen-Mother
—an altogether regal figure, universally honoured and
greatly beloved.

CHAPTER 12

MODELS

As, closing my eyes for a moment, I conjure up the glorious ghosts of those far-off days, one other really Homeric figure presents itself. During my theological course, Dr. Joseph Parker's Thursday midday service at the City Temple was in its glory. It held extraordinary magnetism for students, and, as soon as the last class had been dismissed at College, most of us took the first bus to Holborn. It was a perilous proceeding. Parker was not a good model for budding preachers. His mannerisms—wonderfully effective in *him*—were too pronounced. The shaking of his leonine head; the long pauses that preceded his most telling affirmations; and the thunder of his magnificent voice when, at length, the climax was reached: all this was treacherously infectious. Many a man, sublimely unconscious of Dr. Parker's influence upon him, would be greeted with a roar of laughter in the middle of his College sermon as he betrayed some tell-tale idiosyncrasy that he had obviously picked up at Holborn Viaduct.

Dr. Parker taught me—as also did Dr. Meyer—the high art of repeating myself. I heard Dr. Meyer say identically the same thing on half a dozen different occasions; but he displayed such craftsmanship in his repetition that, unless you had previously heard him say it, you would never have suspected him of having said the same thing before. He perfectly mastered the device by means of which Mr. Balfour so often mesmerized the House of Commons—the trick of pretending to grope for an elusive word, and then, when his entire audience was on tenterhooks as to the missing phrase, he would suddenly hurl it at them with electrical effect. In delivering an address for the fifth or sixth time, he would, at that same point, make the same awkward pause, engage in the same mental struggle and, at length, produce the word with the triumphant elation of a diver who has found his pearl. He said things over and over again; but he said them each time as though he had never even thought of them before.

Dr. Parker repeated himself in the most shameless fashion. And why not? He had no regular congregation: the City Temple was simply a superb preaching station. When he had something great to say it would have been ridiculous—if not actually wrong—to have withheld it on the ground that he had said it before. Of an evening, in the course of our fireside conversations or walks in the Park, we students would often discuss the preachers at whose feet we had sat. On such occasions it was inevitable that we should turn, sooner or later, to Dr. Parker. Very often I heard one student or another tell of some startling thing that he had heard Dr. Parker say: and, more than once, I subsequently heard the great preacher say that very thing from his throne at the Temple.

This discovery has proved of infinite comfort and of incalculable value to me. I am profoundly convinced that the average preacher is too much afraid of saying the same thing twice. If his utterance has savoured of sublimity, let him boldly take its encore for granted. If what he has said was not worth saying, then, of course, it was a mistake to have said it at all. If, on the other hand, it *was* worth saying, then it is the height of absurdity to pledge himself never to repeat it. Only during the first five years of my ministry did I attempt, under pressure of necessity, to prepare two sermons a week. After five years at Mosgiel, I made it a rule to concentrate each week on the preparation of one new sermon. Then, as Sunday drew near, I hunted out one of my earlier manuscripts and set myself so to improve it as to make it more effective than on its previous delivery. All through the years I have proceeded upon this plan, and, if I had my time over again, I should act similarly.

Every good sermon should be given many times. The leakage, in each delivery, is enormous. To the preacher the utterance is so absorbing that he is tempted to imagine that each hearer has caught every word and grasped the full significance of each separate thought. Such is never the case; never! Between his own lips, however eloquent, and the intellectual perception of his listeners there are innumerable avenues for the leakage of his energy. The acoustic properties of the building may not be perfect. The ears of the congregation may not be good. Sultry conditions or defective ventilation may induce drowsiness. And then, even at the best of times, thoughts are wayward things. Minds will wander. Even during the delivery of his most impassioned periods, the men will, in a flight of fancy, slip back to their offices; the mothers will be once more among the little ones at home; the young men and

maidens will be dreaming romantically of each other.
Everything is not heard; and, even if heard, everything
is not fully comprehended.

Dr. Parker and Dr. Meyer taught me that the only
remedy for this kind of thing lies in sane and judicious
repetition. It is the duty of the pulpit to say the same
things over and over and over again. They must be
clothed in different phraseology, and illumined by
fresh illustration, and approached by a new line of
thought; but the things that are really worth saying
must be said repeatedly.

I remember that, some years ago, an idea laid hold
of me with more than ordinary force. It was burning
in my bones. I felt it my duty to give utterance to it
at every possible opportunity. I took it into my pulpit,
and stated it, as effectively as I possibly could, to my
own people. A week or two later I was invited to speak
at a Methodist anniversary. I delivered my soul again
on the same theme; but I noticed in the audience one
gentleman, a prominent citizen and a man of considerable culture and devotion, whom I distinctly remembered to have seen in my own congregation when I first
broached the theme.

A week later I was under an engagement to address
a large public meeting in the City Hall. I once more
harked back to my old subject; and, to my horror, as
I was speaking, I caught sight of the face of my former
hearer. I felt ashamed to be saying the same things to
him a third time. But I thought of the words: '*Jesus
saith unto him the third time . . .*' and proceeded to state
my case as forcibly as I knew how. At the close of the
meeting, as I was leaving the hall, I found my friend

waiting, and not to rebuke me. 'I was greatly impressed,' he said, 'by what you were saying to-night,' and he went on to tell me of what he himself proposed to do in the matter. He gave no hint of having heard me speak on the subject twice previously. Apparently I had then made no impression. Whether it was my fault or his is beside the question. The point is that the leakage takes place, and the wise preacher will make allowance for it.

When, at the age of fifty-seven, I laid down my last charge with a view to preaching over a wider area—geographically and denominationally—than is possible to a man in a fixed pastorate, I deliberately absolved myself from any obligation to prepare new sermons.

'If,' I said to myself, 'if new sermons are born in your soul, welcome them and revel in preaching them! But do not court them! In the course of your ministry, you have prepared and preached sermons into which your heart's best blood has been poured. They are compounded of the very warp and woof of your being. In a word, they are yourself, the essential outpouring of your vital personality, the articulation of your own distinctive message. Deliver those sermons again and again. If you can improve upon them in the process of repetition, so much the better! If, in the course of constant re-delivery, one of them becomes a matter of rote and recitation, drop it on the instant: it is worn out! But, as long as you can preach these old sermons with the zest and relish with which you preached them for the first time, persevere!'

This policy has enabled me to say the things that I am most anxious to say to the widest constituency available to me. It has often happened, of course, that people, knowing that I intended to repeat a sermon with which they were already familiar, have preferred to hear another preacher. Who could blame them? But it has much more often happened that people, knowing that I intended to repeat a sermon which had specially interested or helped them, have availed themselves of the opportunity of hearing it again. And that is all to the good. But, in paying tribute to the lessons that I learned at the feet of Dr. Joseph Parker and Dr. F. B. Meyer, I have run ahead of myself. Let me return to my College days!

CHAPTER 13

LOVE

IN my time the students were boarded out in groups of six or eight. The system may not be ideal, yet it has its advantages. It developed personal intimacy, loyal comradeship and, in many cases, laid the foundations of lifelong friendships. Moreover, it developed in each man the delicate art of harmonizing his own tastes and temperament with those of the men whose room and whose table he daily shared. And it excited a healthy rivalry between the different houses. If a man excelled in classes, in debate, in university examinations or in public life, the glory of his achievement shed a lustre on the house to which he belonged.

For some reason that I have never quite fathomed, the student-pastorates attached to the College were divided among the different houses, and, within the house, were passed on from one student to another in order of seniority. Our house at Durand Gardens, Stockwell, was responsible for two of these student-pastorates—Forest Row in Sussex and Theydon Bois in Essex. Long before I had set foot in either of those charming English villages I seemed to know them thoroughly. And I knew the people who lived in them —at least by name.

For, on Monday evenings, having returned from

our various preaching appointments, we pulled ourselves together for another week's work. And, in the process, we naturally compared notes as to our weekend experiences. And as, in the discharge of his duties as student-pastor, one of the men had, of necessity, been to Forest Row and another to Theydon Bois, we all became familiar with the outstanding phenomena of those two places.

The student-pastorate of Forest Row never came my way. I often spent a Sunday there, mainly because it was near to Tunbridge Wells; and, during the College vacations, when I returned to my own home, it was easy for me to slip over to Forest Row to conduct the Sunday services. It was here that I stayed with Old Bessie, the minister's widow, of whom I have written in *This is the Day!* and other stories.

But the student-pastorate at Theydon Bois, upon which I entered after completing my first year of College life, always interested me. In the course of that Monday evening gossip concerning our weekend adventures, we discussed everything under the sun: the scenery that had charmed us, the homes that had entertained us, the congregations to which we had ministered, and—so human were we!—the young ladies whose acquaintance we had made.

I noticed, from the first, that the conversation invariably took this romantic turn as soon as Theydon Bois came into the picture. I gathered that the student-pastor was usually lodged in a home that was adorned by a most attractive garden of girls. All the men in the house, with the exception of myself, had taken the Theydon Bois engagement at some time or other and were therefore in a position to discuss appreciatively the members of this delightful family. I alone was out in the cold, and I confess that their encomiums piqued my curiosity.

At long last, however, my turn came. The student-pastor was asked by the authorities to preach elsewhere, and the Theydon Bois appointment automatically devolved upon me as being next in order of seniority. I went: I liked the picturesque little village nestling in the heart of the forest: I liked the chapel perched on the edge of the green: I liked the kindness and cordiality of the people: and, quite frankly, I liked the girls. The only fly in the ointment was that one of the girls was missing. 'What a pity,' some member of the household would remark every now and again, 'what a pity that Stella is not here!' Stella, I gathered, both from her sisters and from my fellow-students, possessed attractions peculiarly her own.

A few weeks later, on August 2, 1893, I went to Theydon Bois, not as a mere stop-gap, but to assume the student-pastorate. Stella was there; but, as I was on that occasion entertained at another home, I only met her at the church. The following week, however, I was the guest of her parents. Stella was at the home on my arrival on the Saturday evening. I learned that, after tea, she was walking over to Epping to do some shopping. I saw no sign of any escort: and so, unwilling that she should undertake so lengthy a trudge in solitude, I gallantly craved permission to accompany her. And thus my troubles began. We met with no misadventure on the outward journey. But, walking home through the forest in the moonlight, a vexatious wind sprang up. She chanced to be wearing a very becoming broad-brimmed hat that, buffeted by these untimely gusts, refused to keep its place. It blew from her head again and again. At last I suggested that she should allow me to tie it on with my handkerchief. She demurely submitted, and, as she stood there with the silver moon shining full upon her face, I thought the new arrangement of her millinery even more bewitching than the old. I was thankful that she could not read the daring thought that swept into my mind as, tying the 'kerchief beneath her chin, I looked into her upturned eyes: she would have adjudged her new minister totally unworthy of the nice things that her sisters had said about him. Anyhow, the delicious temptation was successfully resisted and the rapturous moment passed. We saved the hat; but, as we eventually discovered, we lost our hearts. And, since we have neither of us regretted that heavy loss, it seems to follow that the hat must have been a particularly valuable one.

When, on the Monday evening, the conclave of students met in the big general study at the College house to talk over our Sabbatic experiences, I was careful, when my turn came, to raise quite a number of thorny theological questions arising out of my own sermons and out of those of the other men. I was prepared to dilate at great length on the unseasonable weather, on the choice of hymn-tunes, on railway connexions and on autumn tints. On one theme, and one theme only, had I no syllable to say.

In 1894 Mr. Thomas Spurgeon was called from New Zealand to succeed his father in the Tabernacle pastorate. In common with all the other students, I marked this development with deep interest and attended the various services held in connexion with the new minister's induction. I little dreamed, however, that the return of Mr. Thomas Spurgeon from the Antipodes would have the effect of banishing me to the ends of the earth.

On Wednesday, November 14, of that year, however, a strange thing happened. After the morning classes, the entire College assembled, in accordance with the customary routine, for the sermon and its criticism. At the close of this session we sprang to our feet as usual whilst the professors retired, and then gathered up our books and papers preparatory to returning to our various houses. It chanced that my next neighbour on the desk-room benches was F. W. Jarry, who has since won universal admiration by his magnificent lifework in India. Even then his whole heart was set on missionary enterprise and he made no secret of his enthusiasm. On this particular day, instead of rushing out of the hall on the heels of the tutors, Jarry quietly turned and faced me.

'Where,' he inquired, 'are you going to settle when you leave?'

Since I had expected to remain in College for at least another year—possibly two—the question took my breath away. As a rule, a man only hears of a possible pastorate a few weeks before he is invited to it. I had scarcely given the matter a thought.

'Suppose,' Jarry persisted, 'suppose that the whole wide world were open to you, and you were free to settle in any part of it, where would you go?'

'I would go to New Zealand!' I replied on the instant. I was astonished at my own temerity, for the matter had never exercised my mind. But, regarding the conversation as a purely casual and irresponsible affair, I blurted out my reply with that assumption of confidence that is characteristic of young people generally and of students in particular.

'New Zealand!' echoed Jarry, as startled as I was. 'And why New Zealand of all places?'

'Well,' I answered, 'I should love to be a missionary in China or Africa; but there's no chance of that. The China Inland Mission has already turned me down, and no other Society would look at me. That door is closed. Seeing, then, that missionary work is not for me, I should like to go where ministers are few and far between, where men are urgently needed, where one would have ample scope and could lay foundations of his own instead of building on foundations laid by others. I imagine that New Zealand would provide just such a field!'

'It probably would,' Jarry replied thoughtfully. 'We must pray about it!' And away we went.

The next day, on reaching College, I received a message to the effect that, at the close of the sermon-class, Professor Marchant wished to see me in his room.

'Before leaving New Zealand,' the Professor began, 'Mr. Thomas Spurgeon was commissioned by the church at Mosgiel—a church that has never yet had a minister—to send out a suitable man. He has invited the tutors to introduce him to the student whom we should select for the appointment and our unanimous choice has fallen upon you. Will you go? If you are prepared to consider it, Mr. Spurgeon would like to see you as soon as possible.'

I sought out Jarry. 'You knew all about this when you asked that question yesterday!' I exclaimed, accusingly.

'My dear fellow!' he replied, 'I give you my word of honour that I never heard of it until this moment, and I assure you that I never breathed to a soul the confidence you gave me. It certainly looks as if you are being guided!'

I wrote to my father and mother that afternoon. My mother replied by return of post. 'If you go to New Zealand,' she said, 'I shall never see you again. I am afraid we could never consent to it!' After posting that letter, however, she remembered her vow at Prebendary Webb-Peploe's meeting eight years earlier. She therefore sat down and wrote a second letter.

'I am sorry I wrote as I did,' she said. 'We have talked it over and now feel differently. If you decide to go to New Zealand, it will be a terrible wrench. But it may be God's will for you, and, if so, we shall have nothing to say but a fervent God bless you!'

During the next few days everything seemed to be pointing me to New Zealand. Until that critical fourteenth of November, I had scarcely given New Zealand a thought. Of its history, geography and climatic conditions I knew next to nothing. But now! New Zealand shouted at me from all the hoardings; it figured prominently in all the newspapers: it was the theme of every conversation; I met New Zealand everywhere. Everybody seemed to have brothers there or cousins there, or friends who had just been there or relatives who were just going there. The world appeared to be divided into two hemispheres—New Zealand and The Rest—and, of the two, the former seemed to be by far the more important.

As against all this, however, there was one factor that occasioned me a hurricane of concern. I had fallen in love, although, so far as I knew, I had betrayed my secret to nobody, least of all to the young lady herself. How, until I had brought this vital matter to a satisfactory issue, could I dream of leaving England?

The situation was extremely complicated. On the one hand, she was only just seventeen; she was only fifteen on the night of our fateful struggle with the ill-behaved hat. And, on the other hand, I knew nothing at all of the conditions that would await me on the other side of the world. New Zealand was in its infancy; within living memory it had been a wilderness of virgin bush. Would it be fair to say a single word that would commit a girl of such tender years to a life in such a land? I decided that such a course would be unpardonable.

Yet every hour made my duty more crystal clear. I therefore informed Mr. Spurgeon and the tutors that I was willing to go. On December 3, 1894, at Mr. Spurgeon's request, I delivered a farewell address at the Metropolitan Tabernacle, and, on January 24, 1895, I sailed on the *Tainui* from the Royal Albert Docks. On my way to the ship, Mr. Spurgeon gave me a Birthday Book which I still treasure. I handed it round for signatures and among those who autographed it was my college-companion, Jarry, whose unexpected question had first pointed the finger of destiny. Unlike the others, he added a text to his signature—the text in which Paul claims that he has preached the gospel in places in which he was building on no other man's foundation.

And so I left the dear Homeland. My father and mother came to see me off. So did my brothers and sisters, my college companions and many of the people to whom I had ministered at Theydon Bois. And of course, with her father, my Stella was there. Did she understand? Did she guess? To this day I am not sure. The only hint that I allowed myself to give her—perhaps a broad one—was in the actual moment of leave-taking. With the other young ladies who had come to the ship, I probably shook hands. But, in her case, I deliberately and of malice aforethought yielded to the alluring temptation to which I so nearly succumbed on the night on which I wrestled with her hat.

CHAPTER 14

MOSGIEL

OF all the ministers who occupied the Baptist pulpits of New Zealand when I settled at Mosgiel, I have long been the sole survivor. If, as they say, a good start is half the battle, then I inaugurated my ministerial career with a tremendous advantage. A young fellow of four and twenty, I settled at Mosgiel at a thrillingly interesting time. The colony was yet new: the men and women who came out on the first ships were still among us: the spirit of adventure was abroad. Forty-six years before my own arrival, the first two ships had cast anchor in the bay. Those two ships—the *John Wycliffe* and the *Philip Laing*—contained the purest and best blood of Scotland. Chartered by the Free Kirk of that country, and crowded with her sturdiest and saintliest sons and daughters, they were commissioned to found a new colony, saturated in the old Scottish tradition, in the uttermost ends of the earth. The southern extremity of New Zealand was selected for this brave experiment. And nowhere did the spirit of that romantic movement linger more vigorously than in Mosgiel.

It was wonderful how suddenly they vanished from among us, those rugged Scottish pioneers! Some years after our transfer from New Zealand to Tasmania, a minister who had succeeded me at Mosgiel visited us.

'I can't imagine,' he exclaimed, 'where you discovered all the characters about whom you have written. I lived at Mosgiel for three years and I never came across any of them!'

It was pathetically true. In the early days of that first ministry of mine, you could scarcely saunter down the street without meeting some of the original settlers, men and women who had been among the first to land. When I left Mosgiel, twelve years later, their honoured names were all woven into the romance of history. As though the stalwart heroes of that gallant little army had heard a muster-call from some invisible bugler, they set out almost simultaneously on a still more glorious adventure. But it was an incalculable enrichment to have spent those early and impressionable years in their brave company.

It is part of the poignant pathos of a minister's life that the good old men who, as his first officers, fathered him in his callow youth, fall into their honoured graves before he is well launched upon his long career. Like the pilot who steers the vessel through the narrow and treacherous channel to the harbour's mouth, and is dropped as soon as the ship is once tossing on the open sea, those revered fathers in Israel leave the young minister as soon as the initial difficulties have been safely surmounted.

I confess that, as the years have multiplied behind me, I have felt an ever-increasing longing to go back, just for once, to the queer old vestry in which my first deacons were wont to assemble, and to find myself once more surrounded by those rugged old stalwarts, grizzled and grey, who welcomed me to Mosgiel nearly half a century ago. I looked into their faces for the first time as I stepped from the train at the end of my long, long journey from London to that little New Zealand township. They were standing, the centre of a large and excited multitude, on the railway platform in the moonlight; and nobody thought of shaking hands with me until those solemn elders had approached and gravely welcomed me.

How my heart quailed that night as I gazed into their venerable faces! How ridiculously young and inexperienced I felt! But I soon discovered that behind countenances that were like granite cliffs there lay an inexhaustible wealth of human tenderness. They pitied my loneliness, for had they not each of them crossed the same wide seas in the days of long ago? And, deep down in their hearts, I think that each man felt that I had come to bury him, and the thought brought a new softness into all their breasts. During the twelve years that I spent at Mosgiel they, one by one, slipped silently away. I was their first minister, and they were my first deacons. I dare say that the Mosgiel Church has been excellently served by its officers since then; but no group of faces assembled in that vestry could look to me like the apostolic successors of the old men whose faces and voices I still love to recall.

Let me mention three—Wullie first of all.[1] Wullie, a factory operative, had been the church's unordained minister. He was the father of them all. When, on that first night, I stepped from the train to receive their

---

[1] In my books I have invented names for many of the real men and women who surrounded me at Mosgiel. I have thought it simpler—and perhaps kinder—to adhere to these fictitious names in this chapter.

welcome, they all made way for him. His face fascinated me. It suggested both simplicity and saintliness, sweetness and strength. Notwithstanding a certain seraphic quality in his countenance, a boyish mischief twinkled in his eyes. As he clasped my hand, all nervousness forsook me and my loneliness completely vanished. By some occult magic of his own, he made me feel that I was trusted and honoured already. His wrinkled face beamed; his bright eyes sparkled; his speech faltered through sheer emotion. Lookers-on might have been pardoned for supposing that I was his son. I had dreaded that night's experience as the most trying ordeal of my life: he dispelled the illusion and turned it into a homecoming. I was among my own people. One man at least loved me. 'Puir laddie,' he said, as he reflected on my long voyage to a strange folk.

Then there was Gavin. Gavin was severely practical. He had a keen eye for the cutting of the hedges, the weeding of the paths, the painting of the buildings, and all that kind of thing. A perfect treasure was Gavin. He was absolutely innocent of any aestheticism; his one criterion of church music was its volume; he fairly squirmed under a quotation from Dante or Browning. I always associate Gavin with a certain annual church meeting. In order to lure the settlers and their wives from the distant farms and homesteads, we resolved to supplement the business session with a coffee supper. The success of the strategy exceeded our expectations; the place was crowded and the business simply romped through. The evening was quite young when the end of the agenda was reached.

'Before I ask the ladies to bring in the coffee,' I said,

'is there any other matter with which we must deal?'

'Yes,' said Gavin, springing to his feet. 'There is. We ought to have some rules drawn up concerning the lending of church property. Now there are those urns. They are lent to all the organizations connected with the church for their socials and soirees, and the members borrow them for weddings and house-warmings. And nobody cares how they are returned or whether they are put back clean. Now, this very afternoon, when I came down to see that everything was in readiness for to-night's supper, I found half an inch of maggots in those urns!'

It was a most incisive and telling speech from his own point of view, but a perceptible gloom fell upon the coffee supper. It was well for Gavin that the election of officers was over. Had it followed that speech, the ladies who had been busy over the refreshments all the afternoon would have voted against him to a man.

Tammas completes the trio. Tammas was our treasurer; and the man who got church money out of Tammas was regarded in the light of a genius. I can see him now, a massive old man of flinty and wrinkled countenance, with an odd way of looking searchingly at you over his spectacles. I should really have been frightened of Tammas, but he tore all fear out of my heart on the night of my induction. When the solemn ceremony was over and the visiting ministers had left, Gavin, Tammas and I found ourselves standing together at the gate.

'And have ye no coat?' asked Tammas, in surprise.

'Oh, no,' I answered, airily. 'I didn't think I should need it,' and I reached out my hand to say good night.

To my astonishment, the old man took off his own and insisted on my wearing it. If anybody saw me on my way home they must have wondered what horrible disease could have reduced me from the bulk that I boasted when the coat was made for me to the modest dimensions that I possessed that night.

A great theologian was Tammas. As soon as I announced my text, he took a huge notebook from his breast pocket and a stubby blue pencil from his waistcoat. On Monday morning he would be at the manse door looking as though, during the night, the church had been burned down or the treasury pilfered. When the study door had shut us in, he would very deliberately unbutton the big breast pocket and draw out the ponderous notebook with its terrible blue records. I would then find myself confronted with the grim spectres of the previous day's sermons. After I had committed old Tammas to his grave I felt a little ashamed of the manœuvre by which I circumvented this habit of his.

'I can see how it is, Tammas,' I said to him one Monday morning, when his criticisms had been more searching than usual. 'This all comes of trying to preach without a manuscript. I have not had sufficient experience to enable me always to use the precise theological term, and the consequence is that I fall back on the second best, or even an inaccurate one. I see now the wisdom of reading the sermon; such blemishes as these would be less likely to occur.'

I knew that a manuscript in the pulpit was poor Tammas's pet aversion; and, surely enough, the old man came on Monday mornings no more.

I have sometimes wondered whether, during the twelve years that I spent in that tiny township, I missed any strange experience that might conceivably have come my way. In looking back upon that first ministry of mine, it really seems to me that, from being summoned to attend a shuddering felon on the gallows to being commissioned by a too bashful lover with the responsibility of proposing to a blushing maid on his behalf, I tasted every pain and pleasure, sounded every deep and shallow of the ministerial life.

Every day had its own experiences; and every night. I remember, in the early days, being awakened by a tapping at my window.

'You're wanted,' said a voice, 'you're wanted at once at a kisting at 11 Factory Row.'

I sprang up, flung something round me, and threw open the window. The messenger had vanished. Shall I ever forget the bewilderment with which I found myself crossing the fields at dead of night, wondering what weird rite a 'kisting' might be. How was I to know that, in addition to funeral services at house and church and grave, these solemn Scottish folk liked to have the minister present and a prayer offered when the body was lifted into its coffin, its chest, its kist?

The call to a condemned cell came from a prison a hundred miles away. I knew nothing of the horrid case but what I had seen in the newspapers; and it never occurred to me for an instant that I should be drawn into the vortex of its squalor. Returning one afternoon from a visit to a sick child at a distant farm, I found a letter in a large official envelope awaiting me. I tore it open curiously but casually. It was from the sheriff of the gaol. The wretched man lying under sentence of death had sought my help, and the authorities requested me to leave by the first train. The horror of it nearly froze my blood. I do not know how our first parents felt as they exchanged the garden for the wilderness, but I know how I felt as I turned my back upon the fields and farms around my quiet manse, and prepared to plunge into this realm of sordid guilt and hideous tragedy. Happily, the sentence was, at the last moment, commuted; and I was spared the terrible ordeal that, since opening the sheriff's letter, had haunted my imagination night and day.

This, however, was not strictly a memory of Mosgiel. The case was not a Mosgiel case: the people were not Mosgiel people. The nearest approach to anything of this grim kind at Mosgiel occurred on Christmas Day. On Christmas Eve I heard that Jamie Duncan had been found dead in his room. Later in the evening I was told that the jury had pronounced it a case of *felo de se*; and that the funeral was fixed for the afternoon of Christmas Day. In view of the terrible verdict, the relatives declined to follow the body to the grave, and the undertaker refused to lead the cortège through the main streets. On that glorious Christmas afternoon—the midsummer sunshine bathing all the hills in splendour—I alone followed that coffin through the secluded by-ways of the township to the cemetery on the side of the hill; and, when I read the burial service at the graveside, the undertaker and the sexton were my only hearers. I remember that, as I bade him good-bye, the undertaker was kind enough to wish me a merry Christmas, and, somehow, the words sounded strange.

I always felt that Providence let me down very lightly on the occasion on which I was commissioned by Seth Draper to propose on his behalf to Elsie Hammond. Seth was a great fellow, but terribly shy. Terribly shy and terribly lonely. After the deaths of his mother and sister, he had nothing and no one to live for. And, somehow, he fancied that Elsie was lonely, and he knew that she was good. But how to speak to her? In a little place like Mosgiel it might look silly, and people would talk, and not for worlds would he embarrass her. I asked him if he had any reason to suppose that his sentiment was reciprocated.

'No,' he said sadly, 'none at all. One Sunday afternoon a month or two ago I was coming up the road, and, looking over my shoulder, saw Elsie coming a hundred yards or so behind me. She had a friend with her. I had a scarlet nasturtium in my coat. I took it out and dropped it purposely. I glanced back to see what happened, but she only kicked it into the grass by the side of the path.'

The case certainly did not look promising, but I undertook to do my best. On the following Sunday we invited Elsie to the manse to tea. She left her Bible, her hand-bag and her gloves on the dining-room table. To this day I don't know what moved me to it, but, resting on the couch before the evening service, I put out my hand and picked up her Bible. Out fluttered a pressed nasturtium. I decided to draw a bow at a venture.

'Elsie,' I said, when we were alone together, 'Seth Draper dropped that flower; you kicked it into the grass by the side of the road and then went back afterwards, picked it up and pressed it.'

She was covered with confusion, but it all ended happily. Seth and Elsie were married a few months later, and when I left Mosgiel they had quite a little family around them.

And so, sometimes telling of the love of man and sometimes of the love of God, I settled down to work among these simple but sturdy souls, learning at their hands to be a minister of the everlasting gospel.

Chapter 15

MARRIAGE

Early in the morning of Monday, April 13, 1896, we were married, my bride being eighteen and I five-and-twenty. I was, of course, unconscionably proud of her. I have never ceased to admire her courage in leaving her village home in England at such an age in order to sail, quite unattended, to earth's remotest bound and to live a life every tiniest detail of which was entirely unfamiliar to her.

When I left London on that bleak January afternoon, I intended to maintain a decorous and friendly correspondence with my sweetheart, making no faintest reference to my fondest hopes until I had firmly entrenched myself in my New Zealand pastorate. By that time, I argued, I should be in a position to judge as to whether it was the kind of land and the kind of life to which to invite her. This plausible project satisfied me less and less each day. During the six long weeks at sea, the haunting theme monopolized my mind sleeping and waking. In the process, the most delicate problems presented themselves. I realized that, since she was absolutely uncommitted, and perhaps sublimely unaware of the tumult that she had awakened in my breast, it would be the easiest thing in the world for her to become involved in some other entanglement. Indeed, thinking of her as I naturally thought of her, such a tragedy appeared almost inevitable. Who, seeing her, could be insensible of her attractions? Then, surveying the matter from *her* standpoint, I was forced to recognize that, by deferring all action until after my arrival in New Zealand, I was laying myself open to the suspicion that I desired to exploit the femininity of that far field before deciding on the importation of a bride.

Impressed by the cogency of this shipboard reasoning, I therefore resolved upon an immediate overture. When, a few days before reaching my destination, the *Tainui* called at Hobart in Tasmania—destined to be our future home—I posted a private and confidential letter to her father, apprising him of my sentiments and intentions and leaving it to his own discretion as to whether or not he unfolded my secret to the young lady herself.

Having posted that fateful letter and again put out to sea, my tortured mind swung to its normal poise and I was able to concentrate on the preparation of my opening sermons in New Zealand. Those sermons —the manuscripts of which I still possess—were preached on March 17, 1895—St. Patrick's Day. In view of the warmth of the welcome that had been accorded me, and the enthusiasm that had marked those opening services, I felt that any delay in the development of my love affair would be absurd. I therefore wrote the very next day begging my lady-love to join me and entreating her to wire her reply. On the third of May that cable reached me and I was the happiest man in either hemisphere.

How, I wondered, could I break this glorious news

to my people? But old Wullie, my senior deacon, took the matter entirely out of my hands. It chanced that, at about this time, the church found itself in financial difficulties. I do not mean that they had insufficient money: I mean that they had too much. The one paralysing dread of these cautious Scots folk had been lest they should lure a young minister from the distant Homeland and then find themselves unable to support him. This terrifying apprehension, and this alone, had constrained them, through several years, to postpone the realization of old Wullie's darling dream —the calling of a minister.

And now that the minister was actually in residence, the fear became still more acute, with the result that the members contributed with frenzied munificence. The money poured in: the exchequer literally over-flowed: and poor Tammas, the treasurer, was at his wit's end.

'If the church gets to know that we have all this money,' he exclaimed, aghast, to his fellow-officers in the privacy of the vestry, 'the collections will drop off to nothing!' It was generally agreed that, in some way or other, the money must be spent, and each man undertook to think out some means of disposing of it.

But murder will out! At the church meeting held a day or two later, a private member, little dreaming that he was precipitating a crisis of the first magnitude, asked for a financial statement. Tammas rose ponder-ously, the picture of abject misery. Anguish was stamped upon his face. He could scarcely have looked more forlorn or woebegone had he stood convicted of misappropriating the church funds. He confessed, with the countenance of a culprit, that he had fifty pounds in hand! The position was appalling.

But, at that crucial moment, Wullie, as his custom was, sprang into the breach and saved the situation. He rose deliberately, a sly twinkle in his eye, and quietly asked:

'Would the meenister tell us if he has a lassie?'

I was covered with confusion: the cablegram was in my pocket: and I hid my face to conceal my blushes. I confess that, for a few seconds, I lost control of that meeting. But, happily, my very confusion saved me the necessity of a reply. My secret was out. Wullie was on his feet again.

'Then, Mr. Chairman,' he said, with the gravity of a statesman, 'I move that we buy a block of land with that fifty pounds and proceed to build the meenister a manse!'

The motion was carried with enthusiasm. The treasurer looked like a man who had been saved from the very brink of destruction.

The house was built and was for many years my home. It had but one discomfort, and that was the sorrowful reflection that poor Wullie never lived to see either the manse or its mistress. One Saturday afternoon, shortly after his adroit move at the meeting, without a sickness or a struggle, he suddenly passed from us. It seemed incredible. The entire township was in tears. I have seldom seen grief so universal and sincere.

By this time I was absorbed in a whirl of rainbow-tinted plans. On November 14, I received a cablegram telling me that my bride-elect would sail by the

Ruapehu in February. And on March 25 she landed at Wellington, the New Zealand capital. Wellington is nearly five hundred miles from Mosgiel; but I was determined to meet her. As to whether or not I did actually meet her has always been a moot point between us. Here are the facts.

The *Ruapehu* was due on March 24. In those days ships had no means of advising ports of their approach. The only way of meeting a vessel was by haunting the wharves till she appeared. At dawn on March 24, I took up my vigil on the pier. It rained—a steady, misty drizzle—all through the day. I was chilled to the bone and soaked to the skin. When, late at night, I was assured that the boat would not venture in until daylight, I returned to the home of the Rev. C. and Mrs. Dallaston—my host and hostess—for a few hours' sleep. At daylight I was again on the rain-swept pier. In the early afternoon, visibility having become poorer than ever, the harbour officials advised me to go home. 'No captain in his senses would bring his ship through the heads in this weather!' they said. And, as I was again saturated, I acted accordingly.

On reaching the house, Mrs. Dallaston, good motherly soul, insisted on my changing my clothes. Having no other garments with me, she considerately produced a suit of Mr. Dallaston's. Now my good host was of a distinctly *petite* build, whilst I was of clumsier proportions. Recognizing the wisdom of Mrs. Dallaston's kindly counsel, however, I contrived with a struggle to encase myself in the diminutive attire placed at my disposal. My own wet clothes were put to dry.

This transformation had scarcely been completed

when, looking from the window, I descried the tops of two tall masts moving above the roofs of the city buildings. I cried to my good hostess to bring me my dripping suit, and, making no attempt to wrestle with the skin-tight clothes I was wearing, I pulled the wet garments over the dry ones and dashed frantically from the house. A city-bound tram was just passing the door, and, catching the driver's eye, I boarded it. At the very first curve, that hideous tram left the rails and shot across the pavement. How I eventually reached the wharf I cannot now remember. I only know that, by the time I hurried breathlessly on to the pier, the *Ruapehu* had already berthed, and the fond embraces of which I had dreamed a thousand dreams had to be punctuated by laborious explanations and humiliating apologies.

All's well that ends well, however. The laws of New Zealand required that, my lady-love being under age and having no relatives in the Dominion capable of giving legal assent, a delay of three weeks must intervene between her arrival and her wedding. But even three weeks come to an end at last; and, as soon as their tardy course was fully run, we were married. That early morning ceremony, at which exactly half a dozen people, including ourselves, were present, was conducted by the Rev. J. J. Doke. My friendship with Mr. Doke stands out as one of the most beautiful memories of my New Zealand experience. After leaving New Zealand, Mr. Doke became intimately associated with Mr. Gandhi, and, on one notable occasion, saved the Mahatma's life.

In the years that followed, Mr. Doke was often our

guest at the Mosgiel manse and nothing contributed to
the happiness and enrichment of our early married life
more than those memorable visits. In a way we felt
sorry for him. He was so small and so frail; he looked
at times as if a puff of wind would blow him away.
His asthma racked him pitilessly, day and night. Yet
he never behaved as a sick man; never, if he could
possibly help it, referred to his weakness. In all his
movements he was brisk, alert, vigorous, sprightly. He
thought health, assumed health, radiated health. He
emerged from his room every morning with the sunniest
of smiles; whilst, long before breakfast was over, his
clever witticisms and excellent stories would have everybody in the best of humour. His comments on the
morning's paper represented a liberal education. His
mind was so saturated with history and biography—his
favourite studies—that every item in the news drew
from him striking comparisons and contrasts gathered
from the storied Past. The outlook from each window
captivated him. As often as not, he would draw his
sketchbook from his breast pocket and limn some pretty
peep that particularly took his fancy. His home was
luxuriously beautified by the multitude of his oil-
paintings. When he slipped out into the garden, every
flower and bird awoke his enthusiasm. He loved life—
life in every form and phase. In his later days he established a little zoo of his own and filled the house with
the strangest pets. He would tell me in his letters of his
lemurs, his meercats and his monkeys; and of the many-
coloured birds in his aviary. And, as though real life
failed to satisfy him, he invaded the realm of fiction.
He wrote two novels—stories of the Karoo—that, for

mystery and adventure, have been compared with the fancies of Rider Haggard. His lust of life was insatiable. I seldom saw him without his camera. He was eager to perpetuate every scene that confronted him, every experience that befell him.

In addition to all this—and perhaps explaining all this—he represented in his own person the most engaging and most lovable type of masculine saintliness of which I have ever had personal experience. He literally walked with God. He dwelt in the secret place of the Most High and abode under the shadow of the Almighty. God was never far away when *he* was near. To him the study of the Bible was a ceaseless revelry. During his earlier ministry he read it, from cover to cover, four times a year.

I was ten years his junior. He never made me feel that he was presuming upon his seniority; and yet he always impressed me as being intensely anxious that I should acquire, without the toil of patient and laborious search, the intellectual and spiritual wealth that he had gathered in the course of those extra years of pilgrimage. Seated on the broad and sunlit veranda of my Mosgiel manse, he would pour the golden treasure of his mind and heart into my hungry ear. All that he had learned about the choice of books, about systems of study, about the conduct of public worship, about the art of preaching, and about the best methods of pastoral visitation, he endeavoured, in its entirety, to impart to me. And, nine times out of ten, before we rose from our lounge-chairs, he would strike a deeper note. How can a minister keep his soul in rapt communion with God? How can he inflame his personal devotion to his

Saviour? How can he ensure the indwelling of the gracious Spirit? How can he prevent the evaporation of his early consecration, the fading of his youthful ideals? How can he keep his faith fresh, his passion burning, and his vision clear? When my companion turned to such topics, as he often did, his eyes lit up; his soul shone in his face; he would lean forward in his chair in an ecstasy of fervour; he would talk like a man inspired.

I recall a day on which the three of us—the Mistress of the manse, Mr. Doke and I—had just finished afternoon tea on the lawn. We were still toying with our cups when a young fellow rode up on a bicycle. Taking me aside, he told me that Nellie Gillespie, a member of my young people's Bible-class, was sinking fast: it was unlikely that she would last the night. As soon as the messenger had left, I explained the position to Mr. Doke and begged him to excuse me.

'Of course,' he replied, 'but, first, come and sit here beside me.' He threw himself full length in the lounge-chair, his body almost horizontal.

'See,' he said, '*I* am Nellie Gillespie. I am just about to die. I have sent for you. What have you to say to me?'

Entering into the spirit of the thing, I leaned towards him and unfolded to him the deathless story that I shortly intended to pour into the ears of the real Nellie Gillespie.

'Oh, my dear sir,' he moaned, 'you're saying far too much. It's almost as bad as a theological lecture. Remember, I'm utterly exhausted . . . months of languishing consumption. . . . I shall be gone in an hour or two. . . . Make it very short and very simple.'

I began again, condensing into a few sentences all that I had said before.

'Shorter still,' he demanded; 'shorter and simpler! Remember, I'm dreadfully tired and weak! Shorter and simpler!'

I made a third venture, telling in just a word or two of the eternal Love and the eternal Cross.

'Splendid!' he cried, springing suddenly to his feet, and clasping my hand. 'Now away you go, as quickly as you can; and remember, whilst *you* are praying for Nellie Gillespie, I shall be praying for *you*! God bless you!' And the next day he assisted me at Nellie's funeral.

The amazing thing is that, in defiance of the physical frailty that dogged all his days, my old friend laid his bones in a missionary grave away in the heart of Africa.

Being minister at Johannesburg at the time, Mr. Doke conceived the idea that it would enormously enrich the spirituality and increase the effectiveness of his own church, and of all the South African churches, if they had a specific missionary objective, and especially an African objective. He talked it over with Fred Arnot, the renowned explorer and evangelist. Arnot told him of a lonely mission station away up in the interior—not far from the upper reaches of the Congo—that might be taken over by the South African churches and made the centre from which a vast unevangelized territory might be worked. The idea captivated Mr. Doke's imagination, and he resolved to set out on a great trek into the heart of the continent.

His journal, carefully kept to the last, reads like a

section of Livingstone's *Missionary Travels* or Stanley's *In Darkest Africa*. Here, as in those classics, we have the swamp and the jungle, the long grass and the winding trails, the lions and the hyenas, the zebras and the impalas, the mosquitoes and the tsetse flies. His attempts to make the natives of the various villages understand his message are strangely reminiscent of Livingstone. The travellers reached their objective and were given a boisterous welcome. But on the homeward journey his meagre strength gave out and he passed triumphantly away.

My wife and I have always felt that our wedded life received a sanctifying touch at the very outset under the benediction of Mr. Doke's friendship. Life becomes wonderfully sacramental when it is hallowed by such beautiful and heroic memories.

CHAPTER 16

MAORILAND

WE enjoyed New Zealand. Its very novelty appealed
to us. We found ourselves building our nest in a land
of luxurious vegetation and of broad and fertile plains;
a land of sky-piercing summits glistening with eternal
snows; a land of rushing rivers and of thundering cata-
racts; a land of boiling springs and of smouldering
volcanoes; a land of steep hillsides draped with evergreen forestry and of graceful valleys softly carpeted
with a profusion of mosses and ferns.

Here were grouped, in uncanny proximity, the
marvels of which many nations boast. Here were the
sunny skies of Italy and the blue lakes of Switzerland;
the snow-capped peaks of Asia and the rolling prairies
of the West; the hissing geysers of Iceland and the lovely
fjords of Norway. Here, from daybreak till twilight, an
unfamiliar choir of feathered songsters maintained a
constant carnival of melody. And when, at dusk, their
voices faded into stillness, strange constellations globed
themselves around the Southern Cross in the vaulted
dome above.

The life had its weird aspects, for the country is
essentially volcanic; but, to young people like ourselves,
this only intensified the romance. Soon after my arrival,
I went to stay at a mountain farm—a farm that readers

of my books will remember as the home of Granny, one of the bravest of the original pioneers. On a two-horse sledge I was conveyed up the slopes to the homestead on the summit. On retiring on the first night, I was told that the family breakfasted early: I was to lie still till I was called. Being very tired, I consented to this arrangement without violent demur and was soon lost to all the world. I was awakened, however, by a loud noise. It seemed to me that somebody was not only banging at the door, but endeavouring to wrench it from its hinges. I sprang up, struck a match, and consulted my watch. It was just five o'clock. 'If this,' I said to myself, 'is the indulgence allowed to guests, at what weird hour, I wonder, does the family breakfast?' There was no time, however, for nice mathematical computations of that sort. I hastily dressed and hurried out into the great farm kitchen. The daughter of the home stared at me as if she had confronted a ghost. I apologized for having put her to the trouble of calling me. 'Calling you?' she exclaimed. 'Why, nobody called you! The boys are not up yet!' I described the din that had scared me from my bed. 'Oh,' she replied, her face suddenly illumined, *'that was just the earthquake!'* I resolved that never again would I be victimized by a practical joke of that kind. After that I had worse experiences, but they were less humiliating. On one occasion, at dead of night, I left my unsteady bed and, looking out of the window, found the birds flying around the swaying trees and the cattle tearing about the shuddering fields —all in the wildest confusion and distress. But their antics soon ceased. The earth grew still; the starlings returned to their nests among the firs; the terrified cattle became calm; and I stole back to bed.

Again, in November, 1901, on the occasion of the famous Cheviot earthquake, I happened to be staying within the zone of disturbance. How vividly I recall the groaning of the doors and the cracking of the windows! I was standing in my room at the moment, and I remember sitting abruptly down in order to save Nature the trouble, in the course of her frolic, of reducing me compulsorily to horizontality.

Still, although we took this strange land and its people to our hearts, feeling that they belonged to us and we to them, there were times when we endured such torments of homesickness as only exiles know. Many a time, when sitting together of an evening, we would look up from novel or from knitting, and each would catch a glint of tears in the eyes of the other. Without the utterance of a single word, both would understand. For years my dreams were a torture to me. I was always in London at night, either strolling down the Strand or riding on a bus in Piccadilly or catching a train at Fenchurch Street. Awakened by the surge of wild excitement, the stern realities of life in New Zealand would pitilessly confront me and I would burst into tears. Years afterwards, when actually walking down the Strand, or riding on a bus in Piccadilly or catching a train at Fenchurch Street, I would pause, look around and ask myself what there was in such scenes to excite such gusts of uncontrollable emotion. In that prosaic atmosphere, the thing seemed ridiculous. Yet those who have been similarly situated will not marvel.

The fact is that life has a wonderful way of coaxing us into a frame of mind in which we not only become reconciled to our lot: we actually fall in love with it. No memory of my early days on this side of the world is more vivid than the recollection of a horrid terror, a cold paralysing apprehension, that often made me start in the night. I, a young Englishman, loving every stick and stone in England, had come out to New Zealand. Suppose I were to *die here*! My bones to be buried in New Zealand soil! It was an appalling thought, and I broke into a clammy perspiration whenever it took possession of my mind! Later on, another nightmare, just as dreadful, came to keep it company, and I was haunted by the two of them. I married: little children gladdened our home: and we were as happy as two people could be. But suppose, I would say to myself, suppose these children grow up to regard themselves as New Zealanders, totally destitute of the emotions that bring a tug at their parents' hearts and a tear to their parents' eyes at every mention of the dear Homeland! How those ugly thoughts tyrannized me, shadowing even the sunniest of our early days under the Southern Cross!

When, later on, we found ourselves once more in England, we made two startling discoveries: we discovered that England was even more lovely and more lovable than, in our most sentimental moments, we had pictured her. But we discovered, simultaneously, that our hearts insisted on turning wistfully back to the lands in which so many of our years had been spent. The visits Home were, from first to last, a dream of unalloyed delight; we were overwhelmed and touched to tears by the most astonishing kindnesses and hospitalities, yet, in the midst of it all, we found that we had become citizens of the distant south. The wattle and the gum thrust their roots very deeply into one's heart in the course of the years. It is a way that life has, and a very wonderful way, of putting us on the happiest of terms with the place in which we are destined to live and with the work that we have been appointed to do.

Mosgiel itself was a tiny town of about a thousand inhabitants situated on the wonderfully fertile Taieri Plain. Within living memory the Plain had been the bed of a great lake. Shaped like a gigantic saucer, it was entirely surrounded by a circle of picturesque hills. Often in the early morning, standing on one of those green hills, I have seen the lake as the pioneers saw it. For, at dawn, the mists lie so heavily across the Plain that it is almost incredible that you are looking, not at water, but at vapour. And, here and there, the tree-tops, dotting the surface of this spectral sea, appear like boats and thus intensify the illusion.

Some time ago I was watching a cricket match near Melbourne when I felt a hand upon my shoulder. I glanced around and found myself confronting Dr. Alexander McCallum, for some years superintendent of the Methodist Central Mission. He had just returned from a holiday visit to New Zealand.

'I say,' he exclaimed, 'you gave me the shock of my life the other morning!'

I asked him to amplify his accusation.

'Well,' he continued, 'I was travelling by rail from Dunedin to Invercargill. The train stopped at a

wayside station and I got out to stretch my legs.
In walking up and down the platform, I glanced at
the board in order to discover the name of the place,
and, to my astonishment, I saw that it was Mosgiel!
Do you know, I always thought that Mosgiel was your
own invention: I had no idea that such a place really
existed!'

I assured him, not only of Mosgiel's actual existence,
but of the vital part that it played in my own intellectual and spiritual pilgrimage. Looking back upon
them now, those quiet, unhurried days seem like a
golden dream. There were no cinemas, no motor cars,
no aeroplanes, no wireless sets, no distractions of any
kind. It seems incredible to-day that, in that tiny town,
I was able, every Tuesday evening, to muster a group
of eighty young people to a real old-fashioned Bible-
class. They brought their Bibles, their notebooks and
their pencils and set themselves to delve deeply into the
inexhaustible mine of Holy Scripture. I still possess my
own notebooks, with the blackboard outline of each
lesson, and am convinced that, however crude may
have been my efforts to teach these young people, the
study involved in the preparation of those lessons must
have meant a wonderful enrichment to my own mind
and heart.

I can see that old manse still, with the little township
clustered round it and the farms scattered across the
Plain. When, even to-day, I hear of a young minister
going straight from College to a city charge, or accepting
a call to a busy suburb, I covet for him such an experience as came my way. Instead of being run off my
legs by a thousand fatiguing but futile engagements,

I had ample time for reflection, for self-criticism and for study. I was intensely anxious to master two great arts—the art of preaching and the art of reading—and Mosgiel furnished me with a superb opportunity of applying myself to their pursuit.

I had scarcely been a month at Mosgiel before I recognized with shame that, of the real craftsmanship of preaching, I knew next to nothing. People came to hear me and I longed to be able to influence them; but how was it to be done? I felt that my methods were obsolete; my technique was woefully ineffective; the management of my voice was as bad as bad could be. I knew what to say; but I lacked the power to say it in such a way as to arrest, interest and impress my hearers.

I looked about for men who knew how to grip the hearts and to sway the minds of the multitudes that flocked to hear them. I lost no opportunity of hearing Mr. Seddon, the Prime Minister, Mr. T. E. Taylor, a social reformer, or the Rev. L. M. Isitt, the temperance orator; and I attended every criminal trial at which Mr. A. C. Hanlon, K.C., a brilliant barrister, was likely to make his appeal to a jury. On discovering some new device—a telling pause; a subtle modulation of the voice; an expressive wave of the hand—I was impatient for a chance of testing it; and, when the moment came, I watched its effect upon my audience with almost boyish intensity. If I failed to profit from the lessons I thus learned, it was certainly not for want of practice; for what with (1) incessant lecturing tours, (2) my activities at crowded meetings in connexion with the exciting and often turbulent Local Option campaigns,

and (3) the evangelistic missions that I frequently conducted at churches other than my own, I occupied a
pulpit or platform of some kind almost every night.

To overcome a tendency to monotony, I spent hours
in talking my way up and down the scales, sometimes
softly, sometimes loudly, and sometimes varying the
volume of my voice *en route*. My wife complained that
she could never tell whether I had a visitor or was just
giving myself a piece of my mind. I felt strongly that,
since a preacher is essentially a public speaker, no
speaker in any other department of public life should
be permitted to put him to shame. The sublime
splendour of his theme and the awful solemnity of his
ordination vows demanded as great an approximation
to excellence as he had it in his power to make.

In my attempt to acquire the art of wise and
systematic and profitable reading, I was fortunate in
finding a most charming and competent tutor. The
Rev. J. J. Doke, who married us, and who was frequently our guest, was one of the most cultured and
capable ministers I have ever known. I was just
beginning, and was hungry for any crumbs of wisdom
that he, out of his rich experience, could impart. In the
absence of a College education, he owed everything
to the books that he had privately purchased and
devoured.

'Read, my dear man,' he exclaimed, pacing the
veranda in his characteristic way. 'Read; and read
systematically; and keep on reading: never give up!'

'But give me a start,' I pleaded; 'be definite. What
shall I read first?'

He walked the whole length of the veranda and

came back without replying. Then, approaching me with eyes that positively burned, he cried with tremendous emphasis: 'Begin with Gibbon! Read Gibbon through and through! Don't drop it because the first volume seems dry! Keep right on, and you'll soon have no time for bed and no inclination to sleep even if you get there! Follow up Gibbon by making an intensive study of each particular period in which Gibbon interests you. Then pass on to Prescott, Morley and other classical historians. Get Lamartine's *History of the Girondins* and read everything you can lay your hands on concerning the French Revolution, finishing up with Carlyle.'

I bought Gibbon's *Decline and Fall of the Roman Empire* the very next day. I would give a king's ransom—always assuming that I possess such a thing— to recapture the wild excitement of that magnificent adventure. It was my first serious incursion into the world of books. In my boyhood and youth I had read hundreds of books—books, for the most part, about pirates, Red Indians and grizzly bears, followed by a shelf or two of love-stories and other romances of a sentimental kind. But what was this to the glory of Gibbon? I have the volumes still; and if, one of these days, I have either to sell them or starve, I tremble to think that I may by that time have fallen so low as to consent to their sacrifice. None of the tales of smuggler caves, or escapes in the jungle, or fights with sheiks and cannibals had ever fired my fancy as Gibbon did. Every chapter seemed to be a more gorgeous painting on a more spacious canvas than the one that preceded it. My imagination was so captivated by the swaying hordes of Goths and Huns, Vandals and Saracens that I started in my sleep as this imposing and variegated pageant of martial movement swept majestically through my dreams. My unfortunate and long-suffering little congregation were dumbfounded by the discovery that, whether the text were taken from Psalm or Gospel or Epistle, it could only be effectively expounded by copious references to the Avars, the Sabians, the Moguls and the Lombards, and could only be successfully illustrated by romantic stories about the hermits, the caliphs, the crusaders and the monks. Roman emperors stalked majestically through every prayer-meeting address. Mosgiel was as astonished as ancient Gaul had been at finding itself suddenly invaded by the Roman legions! Poor little congregation! They did not suspect that their young minister had burst upon a new planet and that his brain was all in a whirl at the splendour of the discoveries that he was daily making!

Such aberrations, however, were essentially temporary. Sanity returned in due course. I realized the absurdity of allowing my thought to be dominated too slavishly by the book that I happened at the moment to be reading. Step by step, I followed Mr. Doke's programme with incalculable profit. Discovering that the memory does not readily retain passages that occur in borrowed books, I made up my mind to possess myself of each volume before reading it. With this end in view, I pledged myself to buy a book a week and to read a book a week, and I faithfully kept my vow for more than twenty years. In view of the exceedingly modest stipend on which we subsisted in those early days, this system sometimes involved us in a slight economic embarrassment. But, as I shall demonstrate in due course, the books soon began to buy themselves and the task of balancing the household budget was thereby happily simplified.

CHAPTER 17

INK

Mosgiel furnished me with exceptional facilities for indulging that passion for scribbling with which, as a baby in long clothes, the gipsy crone had prophetically credited me. From my earliest schooldays I loved dictations, compositions, essays and all exercises of the kind. My first appearance in print—aside from reports supplied to the Tunbridge Wells papers in the days when, after my accident, I was feverishly practising shorthand—took place soon after I settled in London. I was not quite seventeen when I sent to *The Associate* an article on International Arbitration. The Editor held it for more than a year; but it saw the light in January, 1889. A few months later, when General Booth published his epoch-making *Darkest England and the Way Out*, I, greatly daring, sat down and wrote a screed entitled *Darkest London and the Way In*. A few hours later, glancing down from the top of a tramcar at the placards outside a news-shop, I was electrified by seeing my silly caption staring up at me. I was then nineteen.

I am by no means proud of that youthful effort. The style is ponderous; the phraseology is involved; the diction is lumbering and awkward. But, like that first sermon from which I have quoted, it at least shows that I was taking life seriously. The *Way In* to which the article points is the way of apathy and indifference. It deals with the deadening effects of poverty. The poor may get used to being poor; but, in the process, a moral deterioration sets in. And, out of that moral deterioration, criminality arises.

'The problem', says the article in its closing sentences, 'is peculiarly one for the present generation. Every day is most emphatically telling its tale; and the poor, terrible as they are both in quality and quantity, are daily, almost hourly, becoming worse and worse. Unless the difficulty is at once recognized and grappled with, the matter must soon assume such alarming proportions as to render all hope of recovery vain; and so-called Christian England will owe its moral and social downfall to its own neglect.'

On my arrival in Mosgiel, I discovered with surprise that the little town possessed a local paper—the *Taieri Advocate*—a single sheet published twice a week. On my introduction to the Editor—the Hon. W. Carncross—I pointed out to him that there must be considerable numbers of people scattered about the Plain who regularly read the paper, but who found it very difficult to attend any church. (Those were the days of horse-drawn vehicles and execrable roads.) I suggested to him that such isolated people would appreciate a helpful ministry through the columns of his paper.

'I am sure,' I added, 'that the various ministers on the Plain would gladly co-operate in supplying the matter for a column designed to meet that need.'

Mr. Carncross promised to consider the proposal, and, a few days later, called on me.

'I have decided,' he said, 'to place at your disposal two columns each Saturday. I shall be glad if you will edit that department, securing from the other ministers such material as they can supply.'

I cheerfully undertook the task and, for a while, it worked according to schedule. But the other ministers —delightful men, in whose friendship I positively revelled—were less in love with their pens than I was with mine; and so, most unfortunately for the paper, but most fortunately for me, the thing degenerated into the publication of a weekly sermon from my own pulpit.

Thus, almost from the start, it became necessary for me, not only to write out my sermons, but to prepare the manuscripts for publication. This discipline was, of course, invaluable. It naturally improved the quality of my sermons. It provided me, in a convenient form, with an exact record of what I had said. And it furnished me with a unique opportunity of practising the craftsmanship of letters without forsaking the path of my own ministerial work.

At about the same time, the editorship of the *New Zealand Baptist* fell vacant. The position is an honorary one and is usually held by a minister who adds its duties to those of his pastorate. I was invited to the office. I saw at once that the editorship would enable me to re-cast and re-publish much of the material that I had supplied to the local paper. It seemed as if the stars in their courses were conspiring to multiply my opportunities of acquiring literary facility. During the ten years in which I controlled the destinies of the paper, I wrote, as editorials, most of the essays that were eventually published in *The Luggage of Life*, as well as many that have appeared in subsequent volumes.

Shortly after this—at about the time at which, under Mr. Doke's guidance, I had fallen under the infatuation of Gibbon—a thing happened upon which I can never reflect without amazement. I had been invited to address a Christian Endeavour Rally in Dunedin. I was always glad to be given an opportunity of addressing a city audience; but the trouble was that the return journey was beset by serious difficulties. Trains in those days were terribly infrequent and terribly slow. The ten miles often occupied an hour and a half. A train left Dunedin at twenty past nine, and then, on most nights, there was no other until twenty past eleven. It was extremely difficult to address a meeting in town and to get away in time to catch the first of these trains; yet, if I stayed for the later one, it meant that midnight was a long way behind by the time I reached the manse; and the following morning would be freighted with an insufferable sense of weariness.

On the night of the Christian Endeavour Rally, I had made my speech, slipped out by a side door, hurried for the 9.20 train—and missed it! The thought of a two hours' wait on a draughty station on a bitter winter's night seemed appalling. Looking around for some avenue of diversion, my eye came to rest on the big newspaper office immediately facing the station. Every window was brightly lit: I could hear the thud of the machines: I knew that the *Otago Daily Times* was in process of going to press. Moved by some inexplicable impulse, I crossed the road, walked boldly to the counter and asked if I could see the Editor.

I was astounded at my own temerity. My behaviour seemed entirely out of character: as a rule I would rather write a dozen letters than face the ordeal of calling on a stranger. A few years back I noticed in the morning paper an announcement that the Poet Laureate was coming to Australia. I remarked at once that I should dearly love to shake hands with him. One afternoon, a few weeks later, I had to idle away a few moments outside the Melbourne Town Hall: I had arrived too early for an appointment. As I cooled my heels there, a car drove up; and, before I realized what was happening, out stepped Mr. Masefield. Being in no hurry, he paused to survey the busy scene around him. He stood within a few feet of me. It would have been the easiest thing in the world to have stepped forward and enjoyed the handshake of which I had thought so covetously. But my heart failed me, the moment passed, and Mr. Masefield was gone! For my unpardonable timidity I have never forgiven myself.

On the night of which I am now thinking, however, no such qualms disturbed me. The clerk at the desk politely explained that I had arrived at a particularly busy moment: it was, he added, of no use attempting to secure an interview unless I authorized him to say that my business was important. Nothing abashed, I pressed my request and was ushered into the sanctum of Mr. (afterwards Sir) George Fenwick.

I fancy that, as I climbed the stairs to his room, I cherished some vague notion of suggesting a religious column in the *Otago Daily Times* on lines similar to those on which I was working in the *Taieri Advocate*. Later on, when I knew him better, I actually made this proposal and he cordially adopted it, entrusting me with the editorship of the column. If, however, any such idea occupied my mind on the stairs, I must have dropped it as soon as Mr. Fenwick's door opened. Having apologized for my intrusion, I timidly explained that I had an insatiable penchant for scribbling; that I earnestly coveted the skill that could only come with experience; and that I wondered whether, in the production of a great daily paper like his, there existed any little task that I could undertake.

Mr. Fenwick smiled, uttered a few words of kindly encouragement, and then explained that, having at his command a highly-paid and most efficient staff, he found it impossible to remit any of the literary work to outside hands. Assuring him that I perfectly understood, I thanked him and rose to leave. As I was closing the door, however, he called me back.

'Of course,' he observed cautiously, as though an after-thought had seized him, 'there's always room at the top. The leading article for to-morrow's paper has yet to be written. If *you* had to write it, what would you say?'

It chanced that, at that moment, all the young men of New Zealand were struggling to join the contingents that were being despatched to South Africa. This historic development exactly synchronized with my excitement over Gibbon.

'If I were writing to-morrow's leader,' I replied, with confidence, 'I should establish a contrast between the

patriotic eagerness of these young men to serve in South
Africa and the shameful reluctance of young Romans
to defend the Empire in the days of its decline and fall.'

'That sounds promising,' Mr. Fenwick replied.
'Suppose you sit down and write it!'

Next morning, in the big kitchen of the Mosgiel
manse, a young minister and his wife gazed upon the
leading article in that day's paper with a pride such as
Lucifer can never have known. Thus Gibbon—my first
purchase under Mr. Doke's scheme—paid for himself,
as most of my books have done. For, from that hour,
at Mr. Fenwick's invitation, I wrote leading articles for
the *Otago Daily Times* on all kinds of historical, scientific
and literary themes. And, after leaving New Zealand,
I found ample scope for similar service on other daily
papers. I have written nearly two thousand leading
articles in all. Many of these have become the germs
from which the essays published in my books have subsequently developed. When Mr. Fenwick received his
knighthood, he assured me, in acknowledging my sincere felicitations, that he had often smiled over the
recollection of my invasion of his office on that bitter
winter's night in the long, long ago.

Could any young minister with literary aspirations
have been more fortunate? It may be said that, blessed
with such advantages at the very outset, I should have
given to the world much finer work than I have
actually produced. This, of course, is indisputable;
nobody is more conscious of it than I. Yet, in my
secret soul, I catch myself viewing the matter from
quite another angle. To me, the outstanding and
dominating fact is the obvious circumstance that, but

for those extraordinary advantages and encourage-
ments, I should never have written a line worth reading.
And, that being so, I bow my head, not only in deep
humility, but in speechless gratitude.

I have lost no opportunity of advising students and
young ministers to write as much as possible. Lacking
the incentives that were offered me, the work may be
laborious and even tedious. I recognize frankly that it
is one thing to write with the knowledge that the
sentences that flow from your pen will soon appear in
the bravery of print and quite another thing to write
for the sheer sake of writing. But I know what it is to
write until late into the night with no thought of publication. And I unhesitatingly aver that it is well worth
while.

A man is naturally fluent or he is not. If he is *not*,
the constant creation of manuscript will overcome his
handicap. In the act of writing, the mind is ceaselessly
groping for words. Every word that it captures becomes
from that moment part of its stock in trade. The word,
never employed before, remains within easy reach, and,
when he is speaking or preaching, it will be ready to
his hand. A halting and hesitating speaker will, if he
takes it in time, cure this slovenly and repulsive habit
by persistent writing. The necessity of selecting the right
word as the pen glides over the paper will develop a
facility that will gradually iron out the wrinkles of his
public speech.

Still more should that man cultivate the constant
companionship of his pen who *is* naturally fluent. The
speaker who is gifted with a ready tongue, and who
trusts to it, will be tempted to employ a pound's worth

of language in expressing a pennyworth of thought. Nine times out of ten he will use the second-best word, or even the third-best, instead of the best. He carries the entire dictionary at the tip of his tongue, and, in the brawling torrent of his easy eloquence, he has no time to make a considered selection. For this malady—and it is a serious one—there is but one cure. He must write and keep on writing. As he pores in leisurely repose over his manuscript, he will have plenty of time to ask himself, when each key-phrase is reached, whether *this* word or *that* or *the other* best clothes his thought. The fluent speaker who indolently relies on his fluency acquires the habit of using general terms instead of particular ones. He works to death words like *great*. He speaks of great men, great occasions, great books, great pictures, great poems, great songs and the rest. When he sits at his desk and commits his ideas to paper, he will ask himself in what respect the man or the book or the picture is great, and, using the adjective that expressed the particular type of greatness in which the individual or the volume or the painting excels, he will add distinctive colour and infinite variety to his speech.

In my own case I can claim no credit for having spent so much of my life at my desk. It has been a form of self-indulgence. But, knowing what I now know, I should still write even if I loathed the sight of a pen. For I have discovered in the course of my pilgrimage that the exercise of writing helps a man to marshal his ideas and to present them in the most forceful and attractive way. The preacher who finds the use of the pen irksome and even detestable will display real heroism in chaining himself to his desk; but, depend upon it, he will reap his reward in due time. For sooner or later—sooner rather than later—he will discover with delight that the laborious hours devoted to such slavery have done much to make him a skilful and effective speaker and a good minister of Jesus Christ.

CHAPTER 18

ROMANCE

THE first threads that a man fingers in the course of his ministry have an astonishing way of weaving themselves into the fabric of his entire life. It is forty-five years since I settled at Mosgiel; it is more than thirty-three since I left it; yet I meet Mosgiel in some form or other every day of my life. Let me illustrate my meaning.

After two months on the Taieri Plain I found myself kneeling beside my first convert. She was a girl of about eighteen who had never until then associated herself with that or any other congregation. Arrested by something that I had said on the Sunday, she had come to assure me of her earnest desire to follow Christ. She told her story with deep emotion but with a clear undertone of robust conviction: she made me feel that her reason as well as her heart had been captured.

When, at the next meeting of those grave old officers of mine, I submitted this girl's name as a candidate for membership, there was much lifting of eyebrows and shaking of heads. They all knew her, or knew of her, but not in connexion with any religious propensities. She had earned in the township a reputation for gaiety, vivacity, frivolity. Her sudden craving for Christian fellowship represented an entirely new development and one that must be treated, if not with suspicion, at least with caution. I pleaded in vain that I had witnessed her tears, listened to her contrite confession and heard the agonized cry of her inmost heart. It was of no avail. In their zeal for the honour of the church, these stalwarts felt that they could take no risks. The candidate must be submitted to a probation of three months.

She not only survived the ordeal; she came through with flying colours. Long before the three months had passed, her bearing and behaviour had convinced everybody of her sincerity. At the first Communion service after the expiration of her probationary period, she was most warmly welcomed to the fellowship of the church, and, all through the years of my ministry, she adorned her profession by a life of beautiful consistency and rare consecration.

This, of course, was many years ago. But, quite recently, I chanced to attend a service at which a young lady was set apart for missionary service in India. All who knew her bore witness to the fine devotion and outstanding gifts that she was bringing to her Indian ministry. And, as I listened, I discovered with an indescribable thrill that the outgoing missionary was the daughter of that first Mosgiel convert!

Few things have impressed me more, in the course of the years, than this element of fruitfulness in Christian service. Every word uttered and every deed done has, as the first chapter of Genesis would say, *its seed in itself*; and, although its germination and fructification and multiplication may be difficult to trace, the processes are sure.

There rushes back to mind, as I pursue this line of

reflection, a night on which I was compelled to return from Dunedin to Mosgiel by the late train—the terrible train that left town at eleven twenty. Cooling my heels on the bleak and deserted platform, I felt depressed and miserable. When at length the train started, I found myself sharing with one companion a long compartment, with doors at either extremity and seats along the sides, capable of accommodating fifty people. He sat at one end and I at the other. I expect that I looked to him as woebegone and disconsolate as he looked to me. The train rumbled on through the night. The light was too dim to permit of reading; the jolting was too violent to permit of sleeping; and I was just about to record a solemn vow never again to accept city engagements when a curious line of thought captivated me.

'Here I am,' I said to myself, 'on this out-of-the-way New Zealand railway at dead of night! I can't read: I can't rest: I can do nothing: but I can talk! And there, huddled up in that far corner of the selfsame compartment, is another belated unfortunate who can neither read nor sleep, and who, quite possibly, might like to beguile the time with conversation.'

And then it flashed upon me, not only that I *could* do it, but that I *should* do it.

'We two,' I continued, resuming my comfortless soliloquy, 'we two have been thrown together for an hour or more in this outlandish way, in this outlandish place, at this outlandish time. We have never seen each other before. We shall never see each other again until we meet on the Day of Judgement. What right have I to let him go his way as though our tracks had never crossed? Is the glorious message that, on Sundays, I deliver to my people, intended exclusively for *them*? And is it only to be delivered on *Sundays*?'

The burden of responsibility grew more and more heavy. I could no longer resist the impulse that burned within me. The train stopped for lengthy shunting operations at Burnside. I stepped out on to the platform and walked up and down for a few moments, inhaling the fresh mountain air. I pulled myself together. I wanted to have all my wits about me and to be at my best. The engine shrieked; and, on returning to the compartment, I was careful to re-enter it by the door near which my companion was sitting. I took the seat immediately facing him. I then saw that he was quite a young fellow, probably a farmer's son. We soon struck up a pleasant conversation, and then, having created an atmosphere, I expressed the hope that we were fellow-travellers on life's greater journey.

'It's strange that you should ask me that,' he said. 'I've been thinking a lot about such things lately.'

We became so engrossed in our conversation that the train had been standing a minute or so at Mosgiel before we realized that we had reached our destination. I found that our ways took us in diametrically opposite directions. He had a long walk ahead of him.

'Well,' I said, in taking farewell of him, 'you may see your way to a decision as you make your way along the road. If so, remember that you need no one to help you. Lift up your heart to the Saviour; He will understand!'

We parted with a warm handclasp. Long before I reached the manse I was biting my lips at having omitted to take his name and address. But it was too late: he was gone.

Five years passed. One Monday morning I was seated in the train for Dunedin. The compartment was nearly full. Between Abbotsford and Burnside the door at one end of the carriage opened, and a tall, dark man came through, handing each passenger a neat little pamphlet. He gave me a copy of *Safety, Certainty and Enjoyment*. I looked up to thank him, and, as our eyes met, he recognized me.

'Why,' he exclaimed, 'you're the very man!'

I made room for him to sit beside me. I told him that his face seemed familiar, although I could not recall a previous meeting.

'Why,' he said, 'don't you remember that night in the train? You told me, if I saw my way to a decision, to lift up my heart to the Saviour on the road. And I did. I've felt sorry ever since that I didn't ask who you were, so that I could come and tell you. But, as the light came to me through a railway journey, I have always tried to do as much good as possible when I have had occasion to travel. I can't speak to people as you spoke to me; but I always bring a packet of booklets with me.'

It was my turn to feel some emotion, but there was little time for sentiment. He suddenly prepared to leave me.

'You must excuse me,' he said, grasping my hand in farewell; 'we are nearly there; and there are two more carriages in front into which I have not been. Good-bye!'

And that was the last that I ever saw of him. But

the memory of him has often cheered me with the conviction that many of our daily ministries, apparently futile, are really much more fruitful than they seem.

Another experience into which an element of romance entered concerns the visit to New Zealand of Dr. Harry Grattan Guinness. I had met Dr. Guinness in London, not as an evangelist, nor as a missionary, but as a cricketer. I had watched a match that his opponents must have won but for the fact that he opened the innings for his side and was still undefeated when the last wicket fell.

During Dr. Harry Grattan Guinness's mission in Dunedin, I was unable to attend any of the earlier meetings, but I saw that the series was to conclude with a couple of illustrated lectures, one on South America and the other on the Congo. I promised myself at least one of these; and, on the night of the South American lecture, I set off for the city. The lecture and the pictures far exceeded my anticipations. I was delighted and resolved to return on the morrow.

On my way to the station next evening, I chanced to meet the Mayor of our little municipality. To this hour I cannot tell why I acted as I did; some strange impulse suddenly laid its hand upon me; and, before I realized what I was doing, I was pressing him to accompany me! He was the last man on earth whom you would think of inviting to a missionary lecture.

'You ought to come, sir,' I was saying. 'I went last night, and did not mean to go again; but the lecture was simply splendid and the pictures were magnificent. I am sure you would enjoy it.'

To my astonishment, he accepted my invitation, and, side by side, we made our way to the station. I spent most of the time in the train wondering by what strange impulse I had asked His Worship to join me. That riddle was still unread when we reached the theatre. It was filling fast. Surveying the crowd, we noticed a couple of vacant seats about half-way up the area and slipped into them.

As on the previous evening, the lecture was most interesting, whilst the pictures were among the best of the kind that I have ever seen. For all practical purposes we had left New Zealand miles behind and were in the wilds of Central Africa. An occasional side-glance at my companion told me that he was as interested as I was. Then, suddenly, a change came over the spirit of our dream.

'I propose now to show you,' said the lecturer, 'the photographs of some of the men who have laid down their lives on the Congo.'

I was afraid that this purely missionary aspect of African life would possess less interest for my friend, and I was prepared for yawns and other indications of boredom. The coloured pictures of African scenery gave place to the portrait of a fine young fellow in the prime of early manhood. To my utter amazement, my companion almost sprang from his seat, grasped the back of the chair in front of him, and stared at the screen with strained and terrible intensity.

'It's my boy!' he cried, loudly enough to be heard some distance away. 'It's my boy! That's my boy!'

I naturally supposed that he had been affected by some curious similarity of appearance. Fortunately, his agitation had not been noticed from the platform, and the lecturer went on.

'This,' he said, 'is a young fellow named ——, who came to us as an engineer to superintend the construction of our mission steamer. . . .' The name was the name of the Mayor!

'It's my boy!' he cried, overcome now by uncontrollable emotion. 'It's my boy, my poor boy!'

Neither of us had eyes or ears for anything that followed. The Mayor sat beside me, his face buried in his hands, swaying from side to side in silent agony. Every now and again he would start up and I had the greatest difficulty in restraining him from rushing to the platform to ask more about his dead son. Sitting there beside him, it came back to me that he had once told me of a boy who ran away from home and went to London. 'We were too angry at the time to answer his letters,' he had said, 'and so, after awhile, he gave up writing, and we lost all trace of him.' When the vast crowd melted away that night, I took my companion to the lecturer's room and introduced them to each other. The identity of the fallen missionary was established beyond all doubt, and Dr. Grattan Guinness arranged to come out to Mosgiel and spend the next day with the Mayor and his wife. Which he did.

Within the walls of the manse, also, we had experiences that approximated closely on the romantic. What shall I say of the quarrel between Gavin and Tammas—the quarrel that began at a deacons' meeting and ended in our own bedroom? The scheme that Gavin introduced that night was one that he had cogitated for months. He had worked it out to the last detail. He had plans and specifications and estimates, and, as he enlarged upon his proposals, a look of fond pride came into his eyes. He already saw in vision the realization of his dream and his soul was fired with admiration and affection. He sat back at last, leaving the plans spread out on the table.

Tammas slightly inclined his head and looked at Gavin over his spectacles—always an ominous sign. Then he slowly unbuttoned his coat and drew out the notebook that we all dreaded. He laid it on the table and very deliberately turned over the pages. Then he plied poor Gavin with a fusillade of questions. To make a long story short, he resisted the proposal on two grounds, the one financial, the other theological. Gavin had given no indication as to the sources of revenue from which he expected to meet the proposed expenditure, and he, as treasurer, would never consent to apply the offerings of the congregation to such a purpose. And then, taking out his Bible and consulting his blue notes, he proved from a text in the prophet Amos and another in the Epistle of James, that the suggestion was an outrage on revealed religion. I never saw Gavin more ardent nor Tammas more determined. The position looked to me particularly ugly. In the course of the discussion that followed, some sharp exchanges took place. Gavin gave it as his deliberate opinion that the church finances had drifted into the hands of a niggardly old skinflint who could find a text or two to prove anything that suited him; and Tammas painted in lurid colours the doom of those stewards who squandered their Lord's money and brought wild-cat

schemes into the House of the Lord. At last the proposal was defeated by a single vote. Gavin rose in
anger, stuffed the plans hastily into his pocket, and
strode out of the vestry. I noticed, however, that, in
his wrath, he had forgotten his hat, which still reposed
under the seat that its owner had just forsaken. I knew
Gavin well enough to feel sure that he would not march
home bare-headed.

We concluded the business of the evening about
twenty minutes later, and followed Gavin out into the
dark. The church lay a good distance back from the
road, and a number of ornamental trees adorned the
open space in front. As we walked up the path through
this shrubbery, Davie, the youngest of them all, walked
beside me and commented on Gavin's unseemly exit.
I was on my guard, remembering the hat that, from my
coign of vantage in front of them, I had seen under the
vacated seat. I resolved to sound a note of warning.

'Oh, yes,' I said to Davie, but in a voice loud enough
for them all to hear, 'but we needn't worry about
Gavin; he's all right! He thinks about this church all
day and dreams about it all night. He was here before
you and I ever heard of the church, and I expect he'll
be here after you and I have left it!'

'I'm hearing all that ye say!' exclaimed Gavin,
emerging somewhat shamefacedly from among the
shrubs, and walking off towards the church for his hat.

It was a trifling circumstance, but I could tell from
the tone of Gavin's voice that a work of grace was proceeding in his soul, and perhaps the incident paved the
way for what followed.

I went to bed that night like a man whose bubbles

had all burst, whose dreams had all been shattered. I was excited and dejected and miserable. It was a long time before I could get to sleep; but, when I did, I must have slept very soundly. I awoke with a start, conscious of a light in the room, of voices in the hall, and of my wife in slippers and dressing-gown, bending over me.

'It's Gavin and Tammas,' she explained, 'and they say they want to see you.'

'Why, what time is it?' I asked, rubbing my eyes in astonishment.

'It's twenty to one!' replied she.

'We want to see ye terrible particular!' cried a voice from the hall.

I nodded consent to their admission, and in they came, looking, I thought, extremely penitent. Gavin held out his hand, and, as he came nearer to the light, I saw something glisten in his eyes.

'This is no the way we meant to treat ye the nicht ye arrived,' he said, and he pressed my hand again. Tammas also approached.

'Ye must think as weel as ye can of us,' he said, as he, too, took my hand. 'We shall need all yer patience and all yer luv, and ye must aye teach us better ways. Gavin and I have arranged all about yon plans, and we shall easily fix all that up at the next meeting. Now ye must put up a wee bit prayer for us!'

I crept out of bed and knelt down beside Gavin. Tammas and the mistress of the manse were kneeling on the opposite side of the bed. If the utterance of lowly and contrite hearts is specially pleasing at the Throne of Grace, that must have been a prayer-meeting of singular efficacy and acceptance. Even Tammas wiped his spectacles when he rose. Gavin took his arm to help him along the dark path to the gate, and so ended my first and last experience of diaconal strife.

CHAPTER 19

SHADOWS

THOSE twelve years at Mosgiel were punctuated by poignant moments at the manse. A few months before our first child was born we arranged for a glorious holiday amidst the snow-capped summits and blue waters of the New Zealand lake country. One afternoon we landed from our boat for afternoon-tea on the shores of Lake Wakatipu. Although we carefully extinguished our picnic fire, a spark from it must first have blown into the dry grass of a near-by orchard. We were sued for heavy damages, spent most of our holiday in interviewing lawyers and witnesses, and, although the case was settled out of court, it swallowed up every penny that we possessed—money that we had dreamed of spending in much more romantic ways.

Then, after eighteen months of wedded felicity, a little girl crept into our home, destined herself to become the mistress of a manse. And, five years later, a sister was born to her. This, of course, was joy upon joy. But, following each birth, the mother went down into the valley of the shadow and remained there for many dark and dreadful months. On one occasion, at least, all hope of recovery was abandoned. I shudder still as I recall a day—a few weeks after I had first known the bliss of parentage—on which the doctors, consulting in my study, bade me brace myself for a desolating bereavement. There was, they averred, no hope at all. On the following day—a Sunday—special supplications for my dear patient were offered in all the churches in the neighbourhood, and, to my unutterable relief, those prayers were mercifully answered.

Mosgiel taught me, among other things, the futility of controversy. One pleasant recompense for the natural aloofness of the little town was the fact that busy people in the city found it an attractive retreat. Among those who occasionally honoured our manse with a visit was a saintly old minister—a man of extraordinary vivacity and charm. Everybody loved him. His *father* was one of London's outstanding preachers a century ago; his *son* has since rendered heroic service to missionary enterprise in India; whilst he himself was, in his earlier days, one of Australia's most valiant pioneers. Away up in New South Wales and in Queensland I have met old men whose faces lit up and whose eyes moistened on learning that, in my Mosgiel days, I often drew this Greatheart to my fireside.

I can see him now; his slight and nimble figure; his restless, quickly-moving hands; his eager face with its white, pointed beard; his piercing eyes that caught fire under the excitement that he so frequently displayed. What tales he could tell! And with what eloquence and fervour he would tell them! He held us spellbound for hours at a time. Once engrossed in these romantic reminiscences, he was lost to all the world. The only interruption arose from the intensity of his own emotion. As he told of something that had deeply moved him in the rough-and-tumble days that he loved to recall, his voice would become husky; he would hesitate and pause; and then, rising, would pace the room for a moment, touching his eyes with his handkerchief.

'Forgive me,' he would say, as he resumed his seat. 'Very silly of me—an old man's weakness! But, as I was saying——' And away he would go once more.

None of our visitors were more welcome than he. We became deeply attached to him; loved to hear that he was coming; and, long after his departure, cherished the memory of his stay.

But there came a fairly lengthy period during which no such felicity was ours. Sad to say, I mortally offended him. More than that, I wounded him—wounded him deeply. It was on this wise. We became involved in a newspaper controversy. On some social question, I had, in an official capacity, taken a course which he strongly disapproved. He wrote to the Press, vigorously protesting. So far, everything was in order. I had no reason to be ashamed of *my* action; he had no reason to be ashamed of *his*. I was perfectly entitled to follow the line that I had pursued; he was perfectly entitled to utter his soul in protest. If the thing had begun and ended there, all would have been well.

Unfortunately for both of us, in inditing his protest, he marshalled facts and figures. Some of his statistics, it was easy to show, were wrong. The temptation was too much for me. In a weak moment I replied to his letter, exposing his blunder and pouring all my arrows through this gaping defect in his armour. He wrote again and again, dealing with the general question. To each epistle I replied, disdaining to touch the general question until he had confessed frankly that the figures on which he had founded his contention were false.

The silly thing fizzled out at last, of course, as all such silly things will. But I noticed that, when we met, my old friend treated me with frigid reserve, icily spurning my suggestion that he should return to his chair by our fireside.

I was naturally unhappy. And, being unhappy, the matter preyed upon my mind. The more I pondered it, the more clearly I saw the error of my ways. My official action was unexceptionable; the contention in my newspaper letters was unassailable; and yet—— Who was *I* to write as I had done concerning *him*? I was but a stripling; he bore the honourable scars of long and valiant service; his grey hairs were literally a crown of glory; he had achieved, before I was born, exploits that I could never hope to equal. He had written to the paper on a subject on which he felt profoundly; it was a matter on which I had no deep convictions at all. He had poured his very soul into his letters; my smart replies were simply calculated to pillory him and to make him appear ridiculous.

The affair reached a crisis when I found myself preparing to visit England. I should be away the greater part of a year. Anything might happen to an old man during those months. I was unwilling to set sail with this wretched business upon my conscience. I therefore attended a meeting at which I knew that he would be present. The business concluded, I stepped across to him, took his arm and led him out on to the lawn. I told him frankly that, as to my original action, I had no regrets at all. But,

I added, I had regrets—the most poignant and bitter regrets—at having written to the paper. 'You were perfectly entitled to your protest,' I said, 'and I should have let it go at that.' I asked his forgiveness; he seized my hand between his two; and, always a little emotional, he burst into tears.

Before we left for the Homeland, he came out and spent an unforgettable evening at the manse. It was the most wonderful night that he ever gave us. It seemed as if he had kept all his choicest stories to the last. And when, after supper, I handed him the Bible, he read the One Hundred and Twenty-first Psalm and then led us in a prayer that seemed to enfold us like a benediction during the welter of wandering that followed.

It was the last we ever saw of him. When, returning to New Zealand, I found his place empty, I secretly vowed that I would never again allow myself to become entangled in public controversy. During the years, I have oftened listened to animated debates in which I longed to intervene, and have followed newspaper discussions into which my pen itched to plunge. Straining at the leash, I once or twice violated— in the spirit if not in the letter—my early pledge; but never once without feeling afterwards the pangs of shame and remorse.

Towards the close of 1905, a singular thing happened; the kind of thing that impresses you without your being able to account for the impression. It was a Saturday and I was pottering about in the garden. Suddenly the Angel of the House appeared with a newspaper in her hand.

'Did you notice,' she asked, 'that the church at Hobart in Tasmania has become vacant?'

I had noticed, in a casual way, that the minister of that congregation had resigned; but, as neither place nor people held any interest for me, I had attached no significance to the circumstance. I told my wife so.

'Do you know,' she replied, fastening upon me a gaze of more than her usual earnestness, 'do you know that I have a feeling that *you* will be called to Hobart and that we shall go!'

'But, my dear girl,' I remonstrated, 'I know nobody there, and nobody there knows me! How can you dream of such a thing?'

'I don't know,' she replied, calmly, 'but they'll call you and you'll go! *You see?*'

And, as usual, she was right.

CHAPTER 20

TRANSPLANTATION

INCREDIBLE as it must seem, the invitation to Hobart actually came. To this day I am blissfully ignorant of the circumstances that turned the eyes of the Tasmanian people in my direction. But, be that as it may, the call was extended to me and we were thus involved in a problem of first-class dimensions. Could we bring ourselves to leave Mosgiel, and not only to leave Mosgiel, but to leave New Zealand?

To tell the whole truth, we passed through a long-drawn-out Gethsemane during our last years in the Dominion; and I would do anything in my power to save any other young minister from so excruciating an ordeal. And yet—such is the gracious discipline of life—I learned so much from what I suffered in those days that I would not have missed the experience for all the gold of Mexico.

For the Tasmanian overture was not the first approach that had demanded careful thought. I had been invited to Oamaru, to Wanganui, to Caversham, to Nelson and to one or two other churches. But, after talking the matter over with each other, we had agreed never to leave Mosgiel unless to take charge of a city church. I argued—may a veil of charity be thrown over my youthful conceit!—that, if I once accepted another church of about the Mosgiel size, I should come to be regarded as a man of that measure and no ampler opportunity would be likely to come my way.

In aspiring to a city church, I was thinking, of course, of the four New Zealand cities—Auckland, Wellington, Christchurch and Dunedin. In these I was well known, whilst, so far as I was aware, my name had never been heard in any city outside the Dominion. During the later stages of my Mosgiel ministry, the pulpits of Wellington, Christchurch and Dunedin each in turn fell vacant. In each case my name was introduced, discussed, submitted—and rejected. I felt no resentment. How could I? After all, I was merely the minister of a small country church, and it had become the established practice of the city churches to send to England for their ministers. I recognized at the time that a call to myself would have been a daring and hazardous experiment. Viewing the experience in the mellow perspective of the years, I am convinced that these churches were rightly guided in the decisions that they then reached. And I am no less certain that the discipline of disappointment did me a world of good. At the same time, the ordeal was a little embarrassing and disturbing, for my people at Mosgiel soon heard of the movements in the larger churches and, by questioning me, made my position extremely uncomfortable.

During the Wellington vacancy, I actually received a telegram from the Church Secretary informing me that a unanimous call was certain, telling me of the date of the meeting and asking me to be prepared with a prompt reply. I was at the post office when it opened on the morning following that meeting in Wellington. The fateful telegram arrived a few minutes later. It was to tell me that another issue had been unexpectedly introduced, and that, whatever happened, it was now extremely unlikely that I should be invited.

The city church in which we ourselves were most interested was, of course, the church in the city nearest us—the church at Hanover Street, Dunedin. During a prolonged interregnum, my name was three times introduced; and the speeches made in the city over-night were discussed on the street corners of Mosgiel next day. At last a vote was taken—by ballot and by post—as to whether the church should call me or send to England. We were, at the hour at which the votes were counted, spending our annual holiday at the Nuggets, a romantic little place on the wild Otago coast. The hour drew near that was to decide our destiny, for we both felt that, if Dunedin rejected me, we must either spend all our days in Mosgiel or else leave the land that we had learned to love. On the morning following the closing of the ballot, I walked four miles along the beach to the nearest post office. The telegram was there! With a trembling hand I tore it open. On a poll of some hundreds, the voting was almost equal—so nearly equal as to compel the officers to drop both alternatives for the time being. We behaved, I blush to confess, like a pair of silly children. I began to feel like a much-handled and badly-soiled remnant on a bargain-counter. We spent the remainder of that holiday strolling amidst scenes of the most be-witching loveliness with tears in our eyes and fierce rebellion in our hearts. Yet, looking back upon it all, nothing on the horizon of the past stands out more clearly than the fact that, had our dream been realized, and our desire granted, we should have missed the best all along the line. We can see now, as plainly as if it were written across the skies, that the opening of any of the doors that were then slammed in our faces would have spoiled everything. It would have represented, for us, an irretrievable disaster. Later on, each of the three churches that unconsciously humiliated me in those days did me the honour of approaching me concerning its pulpit. They were delightful people and I could have been perfectly happy with either of the three; but, by that time, I had found my life work; and a return to New Zealand was out of the question.

The unexpected call to Hobart presented an entirely new problem. For it involved, not only a severance from Mosgiel, but a departure from New Zealand. In all our married life we have never faced a question that occasioned us more anxiety than that one. On what principles can a man determine the line of the divine will at so critical a juncture?

I once heard Dr. A. T. Pierson advise the students never to leave one church for another unless they felt both a propelling and an attracting force at work. 'Do not go,' he said, 'unless you distinctly feel a hand pushing you out of your old sphere and distinctly see a finger beckoning you to the new one!' Was I conscious of these dual forces?

I was not tired of Mosgiel; I loved every stick and stone about the place and loved everybody living there. But, after twelve years, I was haunted by the conviction that I was saying very little that I had not said before. Was this feeling, which grew upon me every day, a propelling force such as Dr. Pierson had in mind?

I felt that it would be a wonderful refreshment to minister to a congregation to whom every syllable that I said was new. And it would be an infinite relief to escape the embarrassments that seemed incidental to continued residence in New Zealand. Did such allurements represent the beckoning finger? I could not be certain.

To add to our perplexity, there were two important factors that seemed to bind us to Mosgiel.

The *first* was the fact that, on the very day on which I had received the call to Hobart, I had been elected, on a popular franchise, to the Licensing Committee. The election had caused considerable excitement; every person over the age of twenty-one had a vote and the poll had been heavy; I had announced that, if successful, I would cancel as many licences as the law would permit; and, on this pledge, I had been returned. I felt that my departure from the country before I had completed the task for which I had been elected would represent a dereliction of duty, the betrayal of a public trust.

The *second* serious difficulty lay in the fact that, three years earlier, in 1903, the church had made it possible for us, with our two little girls, to visit the Homeland. In the goodness of their hearts they had granted us leave of absence for six months and had presented us with a substantial cheque towards the expenses of the tour. Would it be fair, after accepting so princely a gift at their hands, to lay down my charge?

The first of these obstacles was easily surmounted. The magistrate who presided over the Licensing Bench assured me that the Committee could sit within three months to decide upon the reduction of licences. The matter in which I was vitally interested could therefore be settled before I resigned my seat.

The other matter was more baffling. If my call to Hobart had been public property, I could have consulted my officers on the point. But not a soul knew of it, and we thought it best to keep the secret to ourselves until our decision had been taken.

For reasons of their own, the officials at Hobart had asked me to let them have my decision not later than Saturday, March 24, and I had promised to respect their wishes in that matter. As that day drew nearer, the issues narrowed themselves down to one. Did the acceptance of the English trip commit me to a prolonged ministry at Mosgiel?

When that Saturday dawned, we were as far from finality as ever. The post office closed at five o'clock in the afternoon and I was determined, come what might, to hand in my reply by then. In my confusion I recalled for my comfort a conversation that, during one of his visits to our manse, I had enjoyed with Mr. Doke. One lovely morning we were sitting together on the veranda, looking away across the golden plains to the purple and sunlit mountains, when I broached this very question: 'Can a man be quite sure,' I asked, 'that, in the hour of perplexity, he will be rightly led? Can he feel secure against a false step?' I shall never forget his reply. He sprang from his deck-chair and came earnestly towards me. 'I am certain of it,' he exclaimed, 'if he will but *give God time*! Remember *that* as long as you live,' he added entreatingly. '*Give God time!*'

That Saturday afternoon, to add to our distress, a visitor arrived. She stayed until half-past four.

'Come on,' I then said to my wife, 'put on your hat and we'll walk down to the post office. We must send the telegram by five o'clock, whatever happens.'

At five minutes to five we were standing together in the porch of the post office, desperately endeavouring to make up our minds. We were giving God time: would the guidance come? At three minutes to five, Gavin, the church secretary, rode up on a bicycle. He was obviously agitated.

'What do you think I heard in the city this morning?' he asked eagerly. I assured him that I could form no idea.

'Well,' he replied, his news positively sizzling on his tongue, 'I heard that you have been called to Hobart!'

'It's true enough, Gavin,' I answered, 'but how can we consider such an invitation after your goodness in giving us a trip to England?'

'A trip to England!' he almost shouted. 'Man alive, didn't you earn your trip to England before you went? Why, you're very nearly due for another!'

I begged him to excuse me a moment. The clerk at the counter was preparing to close the office. I handed in my telegram and rejoined Gavin, who insisted on taking us home to tea. At his house I wrote out my resignation, asking him to call the officers together at ten o'clock next morning. At the appointed hour they were all in their places. They had come to hear what I had to say: as a matter of fact, I said absolutely nothing: I did not even open the meeting with prayer. In my diary I find this entry: 'In the vestry I cried like a baby and wondered how on earth I should get through the day!' Utterance having failed me, I left the meeting, and Gavin said all that needed saying.

On Monday, June 25, 1906, we sailed on the *Waikare* from New Zealand, and on the Friday morning reached Hobart. All the officers of the church were at the pier to welcome us. I somewhat amused them by standing at the top of the gangway, greeting them each by name and introducing them to my wife and children. They insisted that the proceeding was uncanny until I reminded them that, among the documents sent for my information, was a group photograph at the foot of which the names were clearly indicated. In the pleasant atmosphere generated by this trivial incident there were forged a series of friendships that grew firmer and fonder as the years slipped by.

CHAPTER 21

TASMANIA

WE quickly fell in love with Hobart. It impressed us at once as being so very English. The scenery was English; the people were English; the customs were English; whilst the arrival, week by week, of the English boats made us feel that we were in direct touch with the dear Homeland.

Tasmania—an island slightly smaller than Ireland—more closely resembles the Mother Country than any of her overseas dominions. Many a time I have stood on a picturesque eminence just above my old Hobart home, and, surveying the panorama of undulating hills and graceful valleys, broken every here and there by mirror-like sheets of open water, I have fancied myself back in the lake country of Cumberland and Westmorland.

An incident connected with our settlement at Hobart often provoked a smile when we recalled it in the afterdays, although, at the time, it might easily have conveyed to the Hobart people a most unfortunate impression. It happened that our Mosgiel doctor, some time before we left, had strongly advised me to keep a small quantity of brandy in the house in case of emergency, and we had always done so. The small quantity, however, chanced to be in a big bottle, and, amidst the confusion of packing, we decided that it was not worth taking. We could easily replace it when we were fairly settled in our new home.

Pending the choice of that new home, we spent a month at a boarding-house opposite the church, and, during that month, I formed the acquaintance of Mr. Harry Sidwell, a well-known Hobart chemist, an acquaintanceship that ripened into a fast and abiding friendship. Even in those early days we went for long walks together, chatting on every subject under the sun and over it. In the course of one of these irresponsible conversations, I chanced to mention the matter of the brandy.

'Oh,' he laughed, 'leave it to me: I'll get it for you!'

A week or two later we were comfortably ensconced in our own home, and, on the first Friday night—the late shopping night—my wife took it into her head to go down town to see the shops.

'You might call,' I suggested, 'at Mr. Sidwell's: he may have a little parcel for me.'

A couple of hours later she returned, and I inquired with husbandly solicitude as to her impressions.

'Oh,' she replied, assuming a horrified air, 'it's an awful place! Do you know that every shop I entered stank of brandy?'

I did some quick thinking.

'Did you,' I asked, cautiously, 'call at Mr. Sidwell's?'

'Oh, yes,' she replied. 'I called on the way down.' And, delving into the bottom of her basket, she extracted a sodden package containing a bottle from which the cork had become detached! And then we began to wonder what the Hobart shopkeepers thought of the new minister's wife!

It was at Hobart that I found myself. From the moment at which I entered the pulpit for the first time I realized that I was preaching with a confidence and an enjoyment that made my ministry a perfect revelry. It was a wonderful experience to be starting afresh with no old ghosts to haunt me. In the course of a long first pastorate, a man makes all sorts of mistakes, the repercussions of which cramp his movements at every turn. He changes his mind on a variety of subjects and finds the expression of his earlier opinions quoted to him to confound his enunciation of his later and riper judgements. And there is infinite relish in being able to say whatever it is in your heart to say without having to ask yourself how recently you have said something of the same kind. When once I had survived the wrench of tearing up my roots at Mosgiel, and had outlived the ordeal of seeing new faces and hearing strange voices, I discovered that the joys of making a new beginning were immeasurably greater than I had for a moment suspected.

Another factor, and an important one, came into operation. In a country congregation, such as I had enjoyed at Mosgiel, you do not see the forest for the trees. In a city congregation, such as I now had at Hobart, you do not see the trees for the forest. At Mosgiel, if some person of unusual importance—a well-known doctor or lawyer or minister or politician—entered the church, that one outstanding individual dominated my entire consciousness. Struggle against it as I might, I could think of nobody else: that distinguished visitor filled out the whole of my little landscape: I found myself preaching to him and to him alone. The presence of a minister, and especially of an eminent minister, particularly embarrassed me. And shall I ever forget a certain Sunday morning—an Easter Sunday of all days—on which the Secretary and Treasurer of a city church, whose pulpit was shortly to be vacated, made their way down the aisle to a front pew during the singing of the opening hymn? I went hot and cold all over; lost complete control of myself; made the most ridiculous blunders; and found myself groping my way through the sermon in a haze of bewilderment and confusion. The ordinary members of my congregation must have fancied that some painful and paralysing sickness had suddenly seized me.

Of this pulpit frailty, of which I am now heartily ashamed, Hobart immediately cured me. After entering upon that second ministry of mine, I never again experienced any such horrible sensations. Hobart is a city—a small city, perhaps, but still a city—and there were always in the congregation men of the type that, at Mosgiel, had so often unnerved me. Moreover, Hobart is a popular tourist resort; people flock to it from all parts of Australia; during some weeks of the summer the fleet is quartered there; and, as a result, the preacher recognizes at almost every service men and women whose names are household words throughout the Commonwealth.

Under the influence of this new environment, I felt like a bird freed from its cage. I uttered my soul from the Hobart pulpit with an assurance and a delight to which, at Mosgiel, I had been a stranger. Even ministers—my bugbear in the old days—became a perfect inspiration to me, and, the more of them I saw, the happier I became.

At Hobart, as at Mosgiel and, later on, at Armadale, I spent four afternoons a week in pastoral visitation. I found it good. It is good *physically*: the outing and the exercise represent a refreshment sandwiched between the close application of the morning and the public engagements of the evening. It is good *mentally*. It keeps the mind in touch with reality and stores the memory with the throbbing romance of daily life. And it goes without saying that it is good *spiritually* both for minister and people.

During the first three years of each of my three pastorates, I systematically visited, once a year, every home connected with the congregation. On the third annual round, at each place, my wife was good enough to accompany me. Then, after the third year, I concentrated upon the old people, the sick people and the newcomers. Every two or three years I would glance over the list of members and adherents to see if any were being neglected through this process of concentration; and, if so, I looked in on them. But, if a minister conscientiously and diligently visits the three classes I have named, it is wonderful how few homes, for any length of time, are left out in the cold.

One outstanding advantage accruing from our transfer to Tasmania was the fact that it brought me within striking distance of Melbourne, Sydney and the other populous centres of Australian life. Even in those days, one could leave Hobart and be in Melbourne within twenty-four hours; now, by air, I have made the journey between meals. We are not likely to forget our first visit to the mainland. A few months after our settlement at Hobart, the Rev. S. Pearce Carey, the Minister of Collins Street Church, Melbourne, invited me to occupy his pulpit during his holiday in January. He offered, if I cared to bring the family, to place his home at our disposal. The idea of spending a month in a city of a million people strongly appealed to us and we accepted the invitation with avidity. By a remarkable coincidence, our arrival exactly synchronized with the most terrific heat-wave that Melbourne had ever known. For six days in succession the shade temperature soared above 100°, whilst twice it reached 108° and once 110°. Unaccustomed to such fervours, we did all sorts of things that we should not have done. We opened all our windows, thus letting the heat into the house, instead of closing them all securely and thus keeping the house cool as long as possible. We were advised that one of the coolest places in Melbourne was to be found in the shade of the trees at the Botanic Gardens. In poking about among the shrubs, our elder girl found a tap, and, as, in that heat, we were chronically thirsty, we filled a bottle again and again, drinking to our hearts' content. After a while an attendant saw our young daughter emerging from the trees bearing a bottle of water. He inquired as to its source. She pointed to the tap.

'My dear child,' he exclaimed with a wry face, 'you can't drink that! It's Yarra water!'

We *had* been drinking it all day; but, as we crossed the bridge over the Yarra on our way home in the evening, we were careful to avert our gaze from the turbid stream!

Soon after our settlement in Hobart, my literary life entered upon a new and totally unexpected phase. My proximity to the Australian mainland led to my receiving invitations to write for Melbourne and Sydney journals. I contributed a number of freshly written articles, together with some that had already been printed in New Zealand. After a while I received a very kind letter from the Rev. F. E. Harry of Sydney—a minister whom I had then never met. He expressed generous appreciation of my articles and added: 'I was chatting to-day with a number of ministers who were all agreed that your work ought not to be allowed to perish with the papers in which it is appearing. Can you not gather a collection of your articles into a book? We would all do everything in our power to secure the success of such a volume.'

I did not regard the proposal seriously. I could not imagine that there would be any general demand for such a book, even if a publisher could be coaxed into issuing it; and I revolted at the idea of pressing its sale upon my friends on personal grounds. I therefore took no action in the matter; but, in the course of one of my intimate chats with my friend, Mr. Sidwell, I casually mentioned the receipt of Mr. Harry's letter. A few days afterwards, to my surprise, Mr. Sidwell and a mutual friend, Mr. F. W. Heritage, called upon me. Mr. Heritage was an officer of the church.

'We are very keen on this suggestion of Mr. Harry's,' they explained. 'We should very much like to see it carried into effect. We want you to prepare a volume for the press. If its publication involves financial risk, we will take the risk: if it leads to any ultimate loss, we will gladly bear it!'

I was deeply touched by this most friendly overture and generous offer. But I saw at once that it would never do to yield to the request as it stood. If the book were published, and proved a failure, the thought of their burnt fingers would be the bitterest ingredient in the cup of my humiliation. But, in view of their strong desire and practical interest, I felt that I owed it to them to explore the possibilities of producing such a volume. I therefore wrote to the Epworth Press in London enclosing samples of my work.

Three months later I received a reply from the publishing house. The Epworth Press would gladly issue such a volume as I contemplated. The only obligation resting upon me would be that I should undertake to order three hundred copies at half-price.

Three hundred copies at half-price? That settled it! What could I do with three hundred copies? I was prepared neither to hawk them round among my friends nor to give them away. I knew, of course, that Mr. Sidwell and Mr. Heritage would jump at the chance of securing the publication of my book on such terms. But what could *they* do with the three hundred copies? I hated to confront them with that problem. So, without saying a word to anybody, I sat down, wrote to the Epworth Press thanking them for an offer that I felt reluctantly compelled to decline, put on my hat and set off down the street to post my letter. It was late at night and the English mail was closing.

When within fifty yards of the pillar-box, I chanced

to meet Mr. Robert Morris, a well-known Hobart bookseller whom I knew well. It was the sort of night to induce conversation and encourage confidence. Before I realized what I was doing, I was revealing the contents of my letter.

'You don't mean to say that you're declining it!' Mr. Morris exclaimed in astonishment. I assured him that I could see no alternative.

'But, my dear sir,' he protested, 'don't you see what it would mean to me to get hold of three hundred copies at half-price? Post that letter if you dare! I can easily arrange for those three hundred copies; and, if you'll give me a day or two in which to get into touch with mainland booksellers, I have no doubt that I can arrange to take a thousand copies at half-price! Leave it to me; will you?'

I cheerfully agreed; the booksellers ordered the thousand copies; in July, 1912, *The Luggage of Life* was published; and, to my unbounded delight, it made its way through edition after edition and created a demand for a long succession of later volumes.

CHAPTER 22

AUTHORSHIP

At Hobart as at Mosgiel, two children were born to us. After a gap of more than seven years, we welcomed Stella—the only fragile flower in our garden. Then, nearly five years later, came Frank, our only boy. We saw from the first that, as long as she lived, Stella would always have to be coddled and cosseted, the object of constant solicitude, to be watched night and day, treated with unceasing tenderness and guarded from every wind that blows. To make matters worse, our frail little babe sustained, during the first year of her life, a terrible fall, a fall that led to a severe attack of meningitis followed by a long and trying illness.

Did any element of rebellion ever enter our wayward hearts? Were there bitter moments in which we wondered why this had happened to our treasure— and to us? Did we sometimes compare her, enviously, with bonnier girls? Do not press me too closely! I can only plead that, if we sinned, we have most fervently repented. For the little girl who came to us in Hobart has proved a perennial benediction: every phase of our home life has been sweetened and sanctified by the beautiful ministry of her gentle life. If I were asked as to the most nerve-shattering moment that I have ever known, my mind would go back to a certain Sunday morning at Hobart. The service over, I noticed, on emerging from the church, that Stella—then about five—was standing at the manse gate opposite. Catching sight of me, she forgot all about the traffic on the busy street between us, and dashed towards me. As soon as she left the pavement on her own side of the road, I saw that nothing could save her. She stepped right in the path of an on-coming car which, striking her on the full, hurled her, a huddled little heap, into the middle of the roadway. With a horror that I cannot attempt to describe, I hurried across to gather her up, only to find that, miraculous as it must seem, she was quite unhurt. Shy and reserved in the presence of strangers, she has always been to us—and to those who know her—the sweetest and most entertaining of companions: no member of our little circle could bear the thought of life without her.

We had to wait nearly twenty years for a boy. I myself had long abandoned all thought of such a possibility; my wife, on the contrary, never for a moment wavered in her confidence that he would arrive in due course. All through the years she was constantly telling me of the things that she would do 'when our boy comes'. He arrived just before the outbreak of war in 1914. I was at a committee meeting of the British and Foreign Bible Society. Walking slowly homeward in company with my old friend, the Rev. G. W. Sharp, the minister of Memorial Congregational Church, I noticed, as soon as we turned the bend of the road, a car outside the manse. Taking an unceremonious farewell of my companion, I hurried home. Grace, our maid, holding Stella by the hand, was at the gate.

'Stella has a secret for you!' she remarked, lifting Stella up.

'I'se got a little bruvver!' whispered Stella; and so life took on another splash of colour.

Among the personal friendships formed during my Hobart ministry was my friendship with Dr. Robert Dey, the proprietor and Editor of the *Australian Christian World*. One of the magnificent thrills of my early days at Mosgiel came to me when I discovered that I had somehow caught the eye of the Editor of this notable Australian journal. I had hoped that the timid little screeds that I had drafted in my Mosgiel manse might interest a few leisurely people in New Zealand; the idea of their being noticed overseas never, in my wildest dreams, occurred to me. How they came under Dr. Dey's notice I cannot imagine. I have often heard him playfully accuse his son, Mr. D. D. Dey, of having rushed to the conclusion that they gave some vague kind of promise and of having coaxed him into reproducing them, thus involving him in a literary entanglement from which he was never able to shake himself free. But, however that may be, the fact remains that, as soon as, at Mosgiel, I set pen to paper, he began to send me encouraging messages from Sydney; and from that day to the day of his death, nearly thirty years later, he extended to me the hospitality of his columns—a courtesy that his son, Mr. D. D. Dey, has since maintained.

It was not until I visited Sydney in 1912, however,

that Dr. Dey and I actually met. He was about seventy; I was thirty years younger. I was just about to enter a Sydney pulpit, to deliver the special sermon that I had journeyed from Hobart to preach, when he stepped into the vestry and was introduced. He stared at me in mystification. 'There must be some mistake!' he observed. I assured him that I could easily establish my identity. 'Well,' he exclaimed, still looking very bewildered, 'I always supposed that you were an elderly gentleman—much older than myself!' I entered the pulpit a few seconds later feeling thoroughly ashamed: I had obtained by false pretences my high place in the Sydney editor's esteem: nor could I see any way of bringing myself into line with his expectations. But, at the close of the service, he set me at my ease by his cordial handshake and heartening appreciation: I realized that he had quite forgiven me for my tardy appearance on this planet: and we forged that personal link which, strengthened by every subsequent meeting, enormously enhanced for me the joy of living.

No writer ever had a more generous chief. He did everything that an editor could possibly do to elicit the best from his contributors. It goes without saying that no man can be at the top of his form in every line that trickles from his pen. The clock only strikes twelve twice a day. Human nature being what it is, a man must, in preparing some thousands of manuscripts, occasionally fall sadly below the standard of his highest attainment. Nobody knows better than I do that, in my own case, this has been particularly true. Dr. Dey was a man of fine culture, of wide reading and of very rich experience. Many of the things that I thrust upon him must have awakened in his mind the gravest doubts. I can almost see him raising his eyebrows and shaking his head. But that was as far as it went. For, during all those long, long years, he never once rejected or amended a manuscript. And, whilst he kept his critical thoughts severely confined to his own inner consciousness, he never failed, whenever I struck a note that awoke the deepest vibrations of his soul, to write in terms of the most heartfelt gratitude and commendation.

And this leads me to say that, during a long life, in the course of which I have had business almost every day with editors and publishers, I have never received at their hands anything but the most overwhelming courtesy, kindness and consideration. Never a month passes but some aspiring author sends me a manuscript begging me to examine it and to advise him (or her) as to whether it is worth sending to a publisher. To all such beginners I invariably reply: Get your work into the hands of an editor or publisher at once. What is my opinion worth? I may think the manuscript inspired; but, if the publisher sees no merit in it, my valuation is worthless. On the contrary, I may think it the veriest rubbish, but, if the publisher is impressed, my blindness to its merits does not matter. A publisher needs authors as badly as an author needs publishers: if they do not come to him he must go in search of them. Let the aspiring author, therefore, approach the publisher with confidence; and he will find nothing but sympathy and appreciation awaiting him.

One Sunday evening, at Hobart, a thing occurred,

quite unexpectedly, that vitally affected my subsequent life and ministry. All through my active career, I maintained the practice of preaching, during the winter, a special series of sermons, and, if I were starting afresh, I should certainly repeat this procedure. It is good alike for minister and for congregation. It enables a minister, once each year, to follow, exhaustively, a certain line of research, and it gives the people the opportunity of studying the theme of each separate address in the light of the whole body of truth to which it stands related. I had a course of sermons on The Ten Commandments, another on The Strange Stories of the Bible, and others dealing with The Immortality of the Soul, The Doubts of the Average Man, The Furniture of the House Within, The Gospel in Colour, The King's Highway, The Pilgrimage of the Prodigal Son, The Pattern Prayer, An Octave of Benedictions, The Tales that Jesus Told, The Happy Warrior, Sermons from the Seaside, and many similar sets.

On Sunday evening, May 21, 1911, I was embarking, with a crowded church, on a series entitled *The Spectres of the Mind*. The addresses, as the printed syllabus showed, were to be delivered fortnightly. This had always been my practice. It was, I fancy, based upon a feeling that, to pursue the course week by week might expose it to three objections. (1) It would tend to monotony; (2) it would involve a certain amount of strain and concentration; and (3) it might alienate worshippers who could only attend irregularly and who might feel, when they did come, as if they had picked up an odd chapter of a serial story.

During the hymn before the sermon, on this particular Sunday evening, I was deliberating on the precise phraseology with which I should refer to the sequence of discourses that I was about to inaugurate. It suddenly flashed upon me that, by emphasizing the address that was to be given a fortnight hence, I was virtually inviting the more casual members of my congregation to absent themselves on the following Sunday. Could I not say a word that would make the intervening Sundays attractive? It happened that, during the week, I had been reading McGiffert's *Life of Luther* and had been impressed by the way in which the Reformation sprang from a single text.

Whilst I was still engrossed in this brown study, the hymn came to an end and the people resumed their seats. I announced my fortnightly addresses according to the printed syllabus; and then astonished myself by intimating that, on the following Sunday evening, I should commence an alternating series of fortnightly addresses entitled *Texts that Made History*. 'Next Sunday evening,' I added, with the air of a man who had laid his plans weeks beforehand, 'I shall deal with *Martin Luther's Text*!'

At the close of the service, one of my most trusted officers, Mr. F. W. Heritage, came to me in a simmer of excitement. 'That's a splendid idea!' he exclaimed enthusiastically, 'it will be the best series that you have ever preached!'

It was certainly the longest and the most evangelistic and the most effective. And it was the series in which I myself found most delight. It ran—as the theatrical people would say—for one hundred and twenty-five

Sunday nights. Later on, I repeated the entire series. For, on settling at Armadale, I discovered that the Melbourne Public Library could place at my disposal a wealthy hoard of biographical literature to which, at Hobart, I had enjoyed no access. I therefore set myself to a fresh and exhaustive study of each of the personages and pilgrimages involved. In preparing them a second time, I committed them to paper and sent a selection of the manuscripts to Dr. Sharp of the Epworth Press. Dr. Sharp fell in love with them at once and urged their immediate publication. But this presented a serious difficulty.

I was, by this time, producing my essay volumes—*The Luggage of Life, Mountains in the Mist,* and the rest—at the rate of a book a year; and the reception accorded to these ventures was so encouraging that I was unwilling to turn from a line of things in which I had met with marked success in order to tamper with a new experiment. Dr. Sharp saw the force of this objection; but assured me that, if I could see my way to keep up the supply of material, he felt sure that the public could absorb two books a year. And so, for five years, we included a volume of the essays among the spring publications and a volume of the *Texts* in the autumn lists.

Few factors in my pilgrimage have affected me more deeply than the preparation of that long series of *Texts.* The hundreds of afternoons spent in libraries, saturating my mind in the spirit of my hero, attempting to visualize his environment and to catch the atmosphere of his period, were among the happiest of my life. After thridding the intricacies of the hearts of men like

Richard Baxter, William Law, Hugh Latimer and Blaise Pascal, I often returned to my study with my soul aflame. My pocket was stuffed with notes and my brain was overflowing with ideas; but, best of all, I had caught an inspiration which imparted zest to every department of my ministerial activity. The books of the *Bunch of Everlastings* series have been the most successful of all my productions; but, even if they fell from public favour and were entirely forgotten, I should still reflect on all the grace that they poured into my own life and should be thankful that I had been permitted to set my hand to that most enjoyable and fruitful piece of work.

In reviewing my Tasmanian ministry, I often stand amazed at the literary fecundity of those days. I published three or four articles every week; but I wrote at least twice as much as I published. For this there was a reason. One of my most staunch and trusted friends at Hobart was Mr. J. T. Soundy, a man held in the greatest honour throughout the entire community. He was an old man when I became his minister, although, living to a very advanced age, he only recently passed away. A year or two after we first became associated, we were one morning travelling together on the express from Hobart to Launceston. Allowing his newspaper to drop to his knee, he contemplated me curiously for a moment and then startled me with a question:

'How old are you?'

'Thirty-six!' I replied.

'Take my advice,' he answered, gravely, 'and make the most of it! You'll have very few fresh ideas after you're forty!'

He almost frightened me. I resolved to exercise the most diligent thrift in relation to my thoughts. Nothing must be wasted. Every fancy that flitted through my mind must be set down in black and white. I began to write as if my very life depended on the number of manuscripts that I produced. It was not a frenzied activity, for I never wrote hurriedly and never went to my desk unless I felt like it. But the task fascinated me. I despatched, week by week, the articles needed for that week's use, and the balance I packed away in boxes. When I left home on holiday, I wrapped these packages of manuscript in watertight coverings and buried them in the garden! The flames might work their devastating will on the house and the furniture; but I was prepared to take no risks with the precious children of my brain! In spite of my regular output, these superfluous screeds accumulated amazingly until there were hundreds of them! Was their production prompted by a baseless dread? I think not.

The period of sterility was slower in coming than Mr. Soundy had suggested; but it came. I detected no appreciable diminution in my creative capacity until I was well past fifty. But, little by little, there crept into existence a state of things in which I only occasionally added to the store in the boxes. Then followed days in which I had to content myself with writing as many articles as my immediate requirements necessitated. And when, later on, there came spasms of lassitude in which my oracle seemed dumb, I was glad to fall back upon the hoard that I had stowed away. One by one, as my inspiration became more niggardly, the manuscripts penned in livelier years were requisitioned; and to-day they are all to be found in one or other of my books.

To my dying day I shall bless the memory of my old friend. He served me nobly in a thousand ways; but he never laid me under heavier obligation than on the day when, in the train, he offered me this word of solemn warning and of sage counsel.

CHAPTER 23

HOLIDAYS

I CANNOT imagine that I should ever have left Hobart had not the state of my health, which was going from bad to worse, imperatively demanded a complete change. The trouble began with the outbreak of war. People said that I took things too seriously; although it is difficult to see how any man could live through such momentous days without being stirred to the depths of his being. Be that as it may, I formed the conviction that, at such a time, a minister should remain among his own people. I could not bear to think that I might be out of the city when an official telegram arrived bidding me convey desolating tidings to the home of a fallen soldier. When hearts were breaking, and the comfort of the gospel was most sorely needed, I felt it my duty to be on the spot. And so, throughout 1915, I preached twice each Sunday, on all fifty-two Sundays, from my own pulpit, and slept all three hundred and sixty-five nights in my own bed. I do not regret it: in similar circumstances I should probably do the same again. But such concentration, amidst the tense anxieties and poignant conditions imposed upon us by the war, wore me down. Early in 1916 I had to confess that I could not go on. My good people insisted on my withdrawing to Wedge Bay for a thorough holiday.

And here let me say that, both in New Zealand and in Tasmania, we were extremely fortunate in respect of our holiday resorts. In New Zealand we spent one month every year at Taieri Mouth—familiar to readers of my books as Piripiki Gorge. It was one of the most picturesque solitudes in the New Zealand bush. Saturated in Maori legend and tradition, we often came upon the relics of a Maori feast and once unearthed in the sand-dunes a couple of Maori skeletons. Here, to our infinite delight, mountain and river, forest and sea, blended their charms; and, as though even this powerful combination might fail to satisfy our fastidious tastes, a wild, forbidding island guarded the mouth of the river, daring us to cross the swirl of angry waters that seethed between it and the mainland. Only twice did we muster courage to invade its rocky shores. At Taieri Mouth we were monarchs of all we surveyed; very seldom did we see any faces but those of our own party.

At Taieri Mouth a thing once happened on which I can never reflect without a shudder. We awoke one morning to find the bush and the ocean enveloped in a thick, driving drizzle. Our minds turned automatically to the Pirate's Lair—an immense cave running in under the sandstone cliffs within a stone's throw of our holiday home. To it we invariably repaired on wet days. It offered us, not only shelter from the rain, but the sense of being out of doors and in the full enjoyment of our holiday pursuits. Thither, on that bedraggled morning, we went. Now it chanced that our eldest girl —now the mistress of an up-country manse—was then a baby a few months old. During the morning she dropped off to sleep. With a couple of pillows that we had brought for the purpose, we made her very comfortable in a little recess at the inmost extremity of the cavern. She was still sleeping beautifully when the time arrived to return to the camp for lunch.

'What a pity to disturb her!' exclaimed one member of the party who saw us moving towards the tiny sleeper in the recess. 'Why not leave her as she is? There's not a thing to hurt her. And one or other of us can slip down every few minutes to see that she's all right!'

At first we thought the suggestion a wise one, and indeed, we actually left the cave without the baby. Half-way up the slope, however, my wife, moved by some motherly impulse, slipped back to the cavern without saying a word to anyone, and rejoined us shortly afterwards with her baby in her arms. The incident provoked a smile, but no discussion.

After lunch and a brief siesta, we decided, since the rain had set in for the day, to return to the cave. But alas! the cave had passed into history! Whilst we had been enjoying our midday meal, the entire cliff had collapsed, and the seats that we had occupied in the morning were buried under hundreds of tons of sandstone!

Wedge Bay, our holiday home in Tasmania, was no less romantic. Our front windows, facing west, looked out upon the bay. The water was as calm as a millpond and as blue as sapphire, except at evening, when, right between the hills that formed the mouth of the bay, the sun would set over the ocean, revealing a sea of glass mingled with fire. The shores of this lovely lagoon were adorned by scores of sheltered nooks and dainty coves, the homes of the iris, the orchid and the many-coloured heath. The virgin bush, with its giant trees, its flowering shrubs, its delicate ferns and its silky mosses, clothed the rugged slopes as far as eye could reach.

Every ramble in this antipodean Eden held some element of delight and surprise. On Monday, perhaps, our unceremonious invasion of his privacy would startle a porcupine out of his wits, and we would laugh immoderately at the alacrity with which he would bury himself from our gaze. On Tuesday a bandicoot would go jumping up the bank, hiding himself at last in the trunk of a hollow tree. On Wednesday a huge iguana would wriggle in and out of the bracken and stare for a moment, lashing out his long blue tongue fearsomely, but without malice. On Thursday, a kangaroo, taken by surprise, would bound heavily off into the thicket. On Friday, we would come upon a company of solemn storks or a cloud of squawking parrots. On Saturday, we would catch the glitter of a deadly black snake as he vanished into the undergrowth—far more fearful of men than men are of him.

Out on the bay, life revealed itself just as prodigally. The fish were so plentiful and so tame that we often caught in a few minutes enough to satisfy our ravenous holiday appetites for the day. And then, instead of fishing, we just drifted, and, shading our eyes with our hands, peered down into the clear, translucent depths below. And what an aquarium then met our gaze! Those great submarine forests! The sea-floor all studded with bright little anemones! And in and out among this weird fantastic forestry flashed fish of all varieties. Only in waters so rarely visited could such a sight be seen. After a month in this paradise, the memory seemed like a brilliant cinematographic film; and, during the year, on the slightest provocation, our tongues would prattle of the wonderful things that we had seen and done at Wedge Bay.

At Taieri Mouth, in New Zealand, we lived for the whole month on the rabbits that we shot; at Wedge Bay, in Tasmania, we subsisted entirely on the fish that we caught. It may interest dietitians to know that whereas, after a month on rabbits, we returned in slightly poorer condition and found difficulty for a few days in digesting other meats, we came back to civilization, after a month on fish, with weight undiminished or even increased, and able to digest anything.

After the strain of the first eighteen months of the war, therefore, we repaired to Wedge Bay; and, on the very day of our arrival, I slipped on a strip of seaweed, fell heavily on the rocks and broke my leg! The charm of Wedge Bay was its aloofness. It was remote from all the world, out of touch with everything and everybody. All the romance associated with the place suddenly forsook it, however, when I found myself lying there with a broken leg and realized that it might take a whole day, or even more, for a doctor to reach me.

A long illness followed, and I was still making heavy weather of my convalescence when, like a bolt from the blue, there came the call to Armadale. The meeting at which it was decided to invite me was held on the twenty-first anniversary of my ordination at Mosgiel! At first the project seemed unthinkable. How could I tear myself away from Hobart? How could I leave the people who were doing everything in their power to nurse me back to health? I was actually drafting a telegram declining the call when the Rev. Archibald G. Brown, formerly of the East London Tabernacle, intervened. Mr. Brown had been living for some months at Hobart and we had all become very fond of him. He strongly urged me to take my time.

'Do not reply in a hurry,' he pleaded. 'It is by no means clear that your health will permit you to resume the burden of your work here. A change might work wonders. And if you are to have a change, what could be better than Armadale? It is one of the most beautiful churches in Australia; it is splendidly officered and highly organized; you would be relieved of all administrative details; you would have a magnificent preaching opportunity; ample scope would be given you for your literary work; make quite sure that you are acting in harmony with the will of God before you finally decline!'

After a month spent in a torture of indecision, I accepted the call on April 15, 1916, and, on May 21, closed my ministry in Tasmania. We had been just ten years on the island—years so crowded with happiness that, to this day, the memory of them seems like a lovely dream.

CHAPTER 24

EVANGELISM

It was at Hobart that I settled—so far as my own behaviour was concerned—one of the most heart-searching questions that I have ever faced. For at Hobart I found myself in a most intense evangelistic atmosphere; and, whilst that atmosphere was altogether congenial to me, it presented problems. For years I had been groping in a haze of uncertainty as to my own attitude towards evangelistic procedure and evangelistic methods. I had the spirit of an evangelist; I had the message of an evangelist; but I lacked the technique of an evangelist. From the day of my ordination to this day, the one passionate desire of my heart has been to lead my hearers to Christ. I have never entered a pulpit without feeling that, if only the people could catch a vision of the Saviour, they would have no alternative but to lay their devotion at His feet. My soul has caught fire whenever I have exalted the Cross. I have never in my life been so perfectly happy as when preaching on such texts as *God so loved the world . . . Behold the Lamb of God . . .* or *The Son of Man is come to seek and to save that which was lost.* Such themes have captivated my entire being and I have revelled in bringing to their proclamation every faculty that I possess. Yet one thing seemed lacking.

I could never bring myself to follow my pulpit

persuasion by any demand for a visible response from my congregations. I saw others hold after-meetings and invite inquirers, whilst all heads were bowed and all eyes closed, to rise to their feet or raise a hand. I had to confess to myself that, whilst this kind of thing was sometimes overdone, it was often done very tactfully and very effectively. At Hobart it seemed to me that the spirit of the church was so favourable to the attainment of definite results by some such means that I marvelled at my own incapacity to give the method a trial. Yet it was as if my lips were holden: I simply could not do it.

One Sunday night in August, 1908, an incident occurred that stirred all my emotions and compelled me to reconsider the whole question. I had preached to a crowded church on the text: *Benaiah the son of Jehoiada slew a lion in a pit on a snowy day*. The point was, of course, that, even though a man is confronted by the worst of foes—*a lion*—in the worst of places—*a pit*—under the worst of conditions—*on a snowy day*—a magnificent victory is nevertheless possible. It struck me whilst I was preaching that the sermon was, perhaps, a trifle less appealing, from a strictly evangelistic point of view, than most of my Sunday evening utterances. But, for some inscrutable reason, a preacher can seldom gauge the effect of his words upon his hearers.

Having finished my sermon, I announced the closing hymn. During the singing of the second verse, a woman left her seat, slipped into the aisle on my right, and made her way with bowed head towards the pulpit. My first impression was that she was feeling unwell and was availing herself of the exit door in front of her. To my astonishment, however, she deliberately climbed the steps of the lower platform and knelt, in a passion of tears, at the pulpit stairs. I decided to do nothing in the matter until I had pronounced the benediction; but, during the last verse of the hymn, another woman approached from another part of the church, and knelt at the stairs on my left. Immediately at the close of the service, I led them both to the vestry: they both impressed me by their evident hunger for pardon and peace; and they both became devoted and consistent members of the church.

This event—joyous in itself—led me into a quagmire of perplexity. There were some, in whose judgement I had the most implicit confidence, who argued from it that, if I afforded members of the congregation an opportunity of making some outward response, we might witness similar scenes every Sunday night. I recognized the force of this contention; but I saw, too, that another interpretation could be placed upon the incident. For did it not prove that, even though no gesture is invited by the preacher, people who really desire to give an outward indication of their penitence and faith will find some opportunity of doing so?

In this uncertainty, I felt that, by stubbornly refusing to seek an immediate response, I might be grieving or even quenching the movements of the Holy Spirit. 'By persisting in my old course,' I said to myself, 'I may be losing some who might conceivably be won; whilst, by making the experiment, no great harm can possibly be done.' I did not see my way to apply the new method myself; I felt that, since the idea was secretly repugnant to me, it could scarcely be fruitful in my hands; but I had in my congregation a most excellent man who had all the gifts, the experience and the training required for such delicate work. Mr. V. W. Brame had, some years before, been an officer of the Salvation Army: he held an important commercial position in the city, but he retained undiminished his earlier passion for souls. I went to see him, explained my difficulty, and asked him, at the close of each evening service, to conduct an after-meeting. He did it as wisely and as well as it was possible for any man to do it; but we all felt that it was not a success, and, in the absence of its success, we found ourselves returning to our homes on Sunday evenings nursing a sense of defeat that we should never have known had no after-meeting been held. I therefore decided, once and for all, that no man can lay down laws for any other man. I realize the value in the hands of others of the methods that I have never seen my own way to adopt; yet I realize, too, that my own way was the right way *for me* and that it would have been an affectation on my part had I taken a line that, in the very soul of me, I felt to be out of character.

In the years that followed I only twice—twice in one day—departed from the rule I then adopted: and the story of those two exceptions stands as one of the highlights of my ministerial experience. It happened thus.

One Monday morning, a few years back, there came a ring at the front-door bell. Answering the door, I found myself looking into the face of a young minister for whom I had often preached. As soon as he was seated, he approached his business.

'We had a meeting of all the ministers in our suburb on Saturday night,' he explained, 'and, somehow, the conversation turned to our young people's Bible-classes. In each church in the district there is a Bible-class; yet, strange to say, very few of the young men and women who attend these gatherings are members of the churches. The classes meet on Sunday afternoon. So we made up our minds, *next* Sunday afternoon, to get them all together in the Methodist Church, to hold an earnest evangelistic service, and to appeal to them to commit themselves definitely to a life of Christian discipleship and service.'

'Splendid!' I replied enthusiastically. 'I am sure you are on right lines. I shall be eager to hear of your success!'

'Yes,' he continued with, I fancied, a faint tinge of embarrassment. 'But we are all agreed that *you* are the man to conduct it!'

I assured him that he was mistaken. 'You see,' I explained, 'I am already engaged to conduct services on Sunday morning and Sunday evening; and my doctor and my wife are very averse to my preaching more than twice on any one day. And then there's this: you want a man who knows how to make an appeal—a man who will ask these young people to raise a hand or step out to the front or something of that kind. That seems almost essential, doesn't it?'

He admitted that it did.

'Well,' I went on, 'the trouble is that I have never been able to do that sort of thing: it seems utterly foreign to me whenever I approach it. So be a good fellow and get somebody else!'

A cloud overspread his face: I wondered why. He paused a minute and then dropped a bombshell.

'I am sorry,' he faltered. 'I don't know how to tell you. I suppose we ought not to have done it; but we were so confident that you would accede to our request that we announced you yesterday in all the churches. If you insist on declining, we shall be in a very awkward position!'

I laughed. 'You have certainly put your foot in it,' I said, 'but, now that you have gone so far, I haven't the heart to put you to shame. I'll come; and I'll do my best to lead these young people to decision; but don't be disappointed if I ask for no open response.'

He had to be content with that. When I arrived on the Sunday afternoon, I found, not merely the eighty or ninety young people whom he had led me to expect, but an overflowing congregation. The ministers of all the churches were seated on the platform. The sense of interest and expectancy inspired me. I said and did all that I had planned to say and do until I approached the close of my address. Then a strange feeling took possession of my mind.

'These young people,' I said to myself, 'are ripe for decision. They are waiting for an opportunity of declaring themselves. These ministers and workers are hoping that I will afford them that opportunity. And why not? Why not?'

By this time I had reached the closing sentences of my address. The feeling that an appeal should certainly be made had grown upon me as I proceeded. I therefore took my resolve. Having concluded my discourse, I closed the Bible and, turning afresh to the congregation, added:

'There are many of you, members of the Bible-classes and others, who have never yet taken your stand as followers of Jesus Christ. I feel sure that you wish to do so. I urge you to a courageous and immediate decision. If any of you are prepared to yield yourselves to Christ, as your Saviour and King, just rise in your places, look straight at me, call out "I will!" and remain standing.'

On the instant about a dozen sprang to their feet and called 'I will!'

'I shall not prolong this appeal,' I continued. 'If there are others, let them rise at once.' A few more joined the number already on their feet.

'I shall now pronounce the benediction,' I said, 'and then those of you who are standing will please make your way to one or other of the ministers on the platform, handing in your names for church membership!'

The whole experience thrilled me through and through. In my exultation and excitement I repudiated and condemned the considered judgement of the years. The mistake that I had made! Think what I had missed! I would repair the tragic blunder without delay! That evening I was advertised to preach at Footscray. On entering that pulpit I looked around upon my congregation with glowing anticipation. I would duplicate the triumph of the afternoon! I preached the selfsame sermon in the very selfsame way. I was careful to make the various points exactly as I had made them a few hours earlier. I reached the close: I made the appeal: I asked the people to stand

and say 'I will!' Like an academy crowded with statues, they stared at me in stony silence.

I drove home from Footscray that night thinking thoughts that do lie too deep for tears. I had learned in the course of that memorable Sunday that the delicate mechanism of the spiritual realm is not operated by clockwork. There is no guarantee that a certain cause will, on two separate occasions, produce automatically the same results. *The wind bloweth where it listeth and thou hearest the sound thereof;* and only those who are sensitive to the movements of those heavenly currents, and whose ears are attuned to those mysterious vibrations, can enter into the profound secret of celestial guidance and control.

CHAPTER 25

ARMADALE

ARMADALE—the scene of my third and final charge—
is a suburb of Melbourne and a most attractive suburb
at that. It is customary for a student, in leaving
college, to outline in his farewell speech the kind of
ministry that he hopes to exercise. In my own valedic-
tory utterance, I said that I should like to go out to the
ends of the earth, to hold three pastorates, and then
to be in a position to preach, as I might be led, in all
lands and among all denominations. I little thought
that, in His limitless goodness, God would grant me so
literally and so fully the realization of my dream.

I had my three pastorates. And what pastorates!
No man was ever more fortunate. I may be told that
all my geese are swans; but, risking that taunt, I
solemnly declare my conviction that Mosgiel was the
most lovable and romantic country charge in which a
young minister could have opened his career, that
Hobart was the most delightful city pastorate to which
any man could have been invited; and that, of all
suburban churches, Armadale was easily the choicest
and the best. When I published my *Bunch of Everlastings*—the first of the *Texts That Made History* series—
I appended to it the following dedication: '*At the Feet
of Those Three Elect Ladies, the Churches at Mosgiel,*

Hobart and Armadale, I Desire, with the Deepest Affection and Respect, to lay this Bunch of Everlastings.'

That inscription was penned twenty years ago; but the passage of those two decades has only deepened my devotion and heightened my gratitude. If I were starting afresh, I should beg to be allowed to start at Mosgiel; if I were once more a young man of five and thirty, I should look longingly at Hobart; and if I were again a minister in the mid-forties, I should covet, above everything else on earth, a call to the church at Armadale.

Armadale exactly suited me. During my later years at Hobart, I often revolted against the necessity of attending such a multitude of meetings. I felt it my duty, as the representative of a central church, to take part in every helpful movement in the city. I was on every committee and was invited to speak at all kinds of public gatherings. This was all to the good; and, in a way, I revelled in it. But, towards the end, I grudged the incessant drain upon my time and energy: I vowed that, if ever I left Hobart, it would be to assume a charge that would allow me to concentrate on preaching and writing. Armadale presented that coveted opportunity in a superlative degree. The church itself was so perfectly organized that I had no shadow of anxiety about details and arrangements; the week-night guilds and societies ran themselves without any intervention on my part; and the minister was under no obligation to sit on any denominational committee, or join any extraneous organization, unless he himself actually desired to do so.

In writing this, it is in my heart to offer one modest

word of personal testimony. My pilgrimage has taught me many things; but it has made nothing more clear than the fact that, from those who humbly seek the leadership of the Kindly Light, the divine guidance is never withheld. In the course of my life I have had to make some momentous decisions—momentous to me— but, looking back along the road, I can now see clearly that, at every crisis, I was rightly led. Whenever the road forked, I heard a voice saying: '*This is the way, walk ye in it!*'

I learned this lesson at the outset and it has been often reinforced. Let me interpolate a pair of instances —one from my earlier ministry and one from my later—to make clear my meaning. I remember sitting, late one snowy afternoon, in my Mosgiel study. I had been visiting and was very tired. Suddenly there came a ring at the bell. I answered the door myself. Flora Harris, of Saddle Hill, was desperately ill: could I go at once? The man who brought the message would drive me to the house, if I did not mind walking back or trusting to the chance of a lift. I looked at my watch: it was five o'clock: and I had a Bible-class at half-past seven. However, I slipped on my coat and set out. Flora was very weak; she was to some extent under the influence of an opiate; and I had to wait some time before I could hold intelligent conversation with her.

It was half-past six when I left the house. Snow whitened all the ground. As I descended the hill that led to the main road I heard the clatter of hoofs and the rattle of wheels in the distance. It was a clear, frosty evening and I knew that the vehicle must be some distance away. It was evidently somebody driving towards Mosgiel. If only I could reach the main road before he passed, I should be spared a long and tiring walk; I should have time for a cup of tea before taking my class; and I should be fresh instead of weary when class-time came. I hurried and, in my simplicity, I lifted up my heart in prayer, asking that the driver of the approaching vehicle might catch sight of my hurrying form or hear my call. But, when I was within a hundred yards of the high road, the vehicle flashed by. I recognized it. It was Willie Brown's: he was alone: and, had he seen or heard me, he would gladly have driven me home. I felt vexed. Of what practical use is prayer? Guidance fails when it is most needed! I set out to walk home and, half a mile down the road, came upon the vehicle I had so narrowly missed. The horse was lying with a broken leg doubled up under it: the buggy was completely wrecked: and Willie Brown was stretched out unconscious beside it. I hastened to the nearest house, sent a boy on a bicycle for the doctor, and eventually reached home in the doctor's gig in time for a cup of tea and for my class. With shame I reflected—and have many a time reflected since—that we are often guided when we least suspect it.

The story from my later ministry has to do with a certain Saturday on which a policeman came to the front door just before noon. A man under arrest at the Melbourne Gaol wished to see me at once. The constable gave me the man's name, but it conveyed nothing to me. My first impulse was to hurry away to the gaol; and, indeed, the policeman urged this course upon me. On the other hand, an appetizing dinner was almost ready, and the cricket match at which I had expected to spend the afternoon was at a particularly exciting stage.

As I pondered the situation in which I found myself, an irresistible conviction settled down upon me that I should be wise to have my dinner in peace, to attend the cricket match to which I had looked forward, and then to go to the gaol in the evening. The policeman protested that Saturday night would be the worst possible time at which to visit the Melbourne Gaol; but the feeling in my mind would not be shaken off. Let me say in self-defence that I can recall no other case in which I put apparently selfish considerations before the clamant call of duty. But my mind was fixed. I ate my dinner and made my way to the cricket ground. In the pavilion I sat beside a man with whom I had been acquainted many years before in Tasmania.

'I don't know why I've come here to-day,' he said. 'I've never been here before, and I take very little interest in cricket!'

To my utter amazement, in the course of casual conversation, he mentioned the name of the man in the Melbourne Gaol. I concealed my intense interest, but gently encouraged him to talk. In the course of half an hour I had all the facts of the case at my fingers' ends; and, when I went to the gaol that night, I was able to deal with the man in a way that, but for my experience in the afternoon, would have been impossible. Now, why was my old Tasmanian friend so strongly moved to visit that particular cricket ground that afternoon? And why was I made to feel so deeply that I must go to the cricket match before responding to the prisoner's call?

The pillar of cloud in the daytime and the pillar of fire in the night never fail. I have, in my time, received many calls to vacant pulpits, some of which occasioned my wife and myself the most anxious thought. Distrusting alike our own discernment and the judgement of others, we have earnestly sought a heavenly illumination of our enshrouded path. And to-day, viewing our former perplexities in grateful retrospect, we can see, as clearly as it is possible to see anything, that we were right in declining the calls that we declined and right in accepting the invitations to Mosgiel, Hobart and Armadale.

We had scarcely settled at Armadale when our last child was born. A few days before her birth we were so troubled about her chances of a propitious arrival and survival that I walked round to see the doctor. I told him of our anxiety. The whole period during which we had been expecting her had, I explained, been a period of ceaseless worry and disturbance. There had been my accident at Wedge Bay; the inevitable shock to my poor wife, who was with me when I fell and upon whom all the responsibilities of a trying situation devolved; the long illness that followed the accident—the illness in which she, of necessity, had been chief nurse; then the month of mental torture precipitated by the call to Armadale; and finally the breaking up of the Hobart home, the wrench of ceaseless farewells, the sale of furniture, the sea voyage, the settlement among strangers, and the strain of house-hunting and refurnishing.

'What kind of a child can this be?' I asked Dr. Davies in alarm. With that fine sanity that he has always mingled with helpful sympathy and unfailing skill, he laughed his reassuring reply.

'The child will probably be the bonniest and healthiest that you have had!' he answered.

And so it turned out. Like the medieval saint, we can testify that we have had many and great troubles in our time, but *most of them never happened!* Thus our little family of five was completed. They are all living, and, to our great joy, each is happily occupied with some form of Christian service.

If, at Armadale, we gained a daughter, we also lost one. For there our eldest girl was married. I myself officiated at the wedding whilst her brother— a brave young knight of eight summers—gave the bride away. If the happy pair have nothing else in common, they at least share a common birthday. For the bride and her bridegroom—the Rev. Norman T. McDonald, a Presbyterian minister—were both born on the twenty-seventh of September, and on the twenty-seventh of September they were married. Their manse is now the home of our three little grand-daughters.

CHAPTER 26

AUTUMN

THERE are two features of my Armadale ministry on which I love to dwell. The first is my Sunday evening congregation. At my induction in 1916, one of the speakers was the Rev. David Millar of the Presbyterian Church. In the course of some very kind words of welcome, Mr. Millar remarked on the extreme difficulty of gathering a Sunday evening congregation in that particular district. 'One thing is certain,' Mr. Millar added, 'and it is this: if this new minister of yours succeeds in attracting an evening congregation, no neighbouring minister will be able to charge him with sheep-stealing, for we none of us have congregations on Sunday nights.' At first blush, the utterance filled me with dismay, for both at Mosgiel and at Hobart I had specialized, not altogether without success, on my Sunday evening work. But, on reflection, I resolved to regard Mr. Millar's speech as a challenge. I issued my syllabus of special subjects, and called for a hundred volunteers to distribute copies from house to house. As at Hobart, I called these hundred people together for prayer and conference before they commenced their work. I laid down certain essential principles. (1) On no account was the syllabus to be placed in a letter-box or slipped under a door or delivered to a child. If the people of the house were not at home, the worker was to call a second and, if necessary, a third time so that a personal assurance of welcome might accompany the printed programme. (2) The visitor was to memorize the names and faces of the people on whom he called, to watch for them at the services, to welcome them when they appeared and to report to me. (3) Half-way through the course, if the people visited had made no appearance at the church, a further call was to be made. It goes without saying that, whenever people explained that they were already associated with some other congregation, the visitor was to express our greetings and best wishes for the minister and church concerned and let the matter drop. The workers completed their task bravely, with gratifying results.

I soon discovered that the people who composed my evening congregation at Armadale possessed idiosyncrasies that were new to me. At Mosgiel and at Hobart, when individuals or groups had attended the church several times, I took steps to obtain their names and addresses, following this procedure with a visit. This approach, invariably welcomed, often led to a closer relationship between the new worshippers and the church. But at Armadale such a policy was fatal. Most of the people liked to come and go without having the slightest notice taken of them. Display the faintest shadow of curiosity or interest, and you would see their faces no more. In an attempt to display friendliness without outraging this reticence, I had a dainty little card printed. The card simply expressed our gratification that the recipient was now attending the services: it assured him of our eagerness to cultivate his acquaintance and show him any attention in our power: and it invited him, if he were willing that the minister should call, to write his name and address on the back of the card and to leave it with the officers at the door on the occasion of his next attendance.

We agreed to distribute the cards at the close of the first service that was really crowded, so as to catch as many strangers at one stroke as possible. On a certain Sunday evening, shortly afterwards, the church was absolutely packed: the cards were distributed as the people left the building: and the following Sunday, although all the conditions were conducive to a large attendance, we had one of the poorest congregations on record! From that time forth we yielded to the inevitable and let the people have their own way!

The other feature of my Victorian ministry that, in retrospect, specially interests me, has to do with the week-night service. When I first settled at Armadale, I proceeded along the lines that I had always followed— prepared one new sermon each week, revised one old one and prepared a little homily, sometimes new and sometimes old, for the service on Wednesday evening. After a year or two at Armadale, I became afflicted with doubts as to the value of this third utterance. Can any man assimilate three set sermons a week? As I looked round upon my week-night congregation, I realized that most of the faces were tired faces. Few of these folk were in the mood to follow a carefully reasoned disquisition; their countenances only brightened when I employed some striking illustration or introduced a gleam of humour. I decided to drop the address altogether.

Instead, I kept my ears wide open, in the course of visitation or ordinary conversation, for interesting narratives of conversion, of answered prayer or of some phase of spiritual experience. When a story of this kind was told me—and every minister listens to some such recital almost daily—I would say: 'My dear sir, you must tell that story on Wednesday evening!' Those who shrank from public utterance, I coaxed into writing a letter that I could read at the meeting. As soon as the speaker had told his story, or the letter had been read, I would announce a hymn, remarking, as I did so, that I felt sure that others present had enjoyed a similar experience: if so, they could tell us about it when the hymn had been sung. Following this practice, we had some most delightful and profitable gatherings. It is always good for a man to unfold to others the work of God in his own soul, and it is always a means of grace to listen to such moving narratives.

At Armadale we acquired two habits that, in retrospect, afford us the greatest satisfaction. I confidently commend them to all ministers.

(1) We made it our custom to go to bed every day after lunch. I do not mean forty winks on a chair or a sofa. We undressed, went to bed, and, as a rule, slept soundly. It is an excellent thing to do, especially for those whose most exacting duties occupy the evening hours. It can easily be done. Lunch is over, say, at half-past one. Nobody wants to be visited until half-past two or three. Why not make the most of this providential breathing space?

(2) We set aside Thursday afternoon for an outing

by our two selves. Every Thursday afternoon, for
thirteen years, we set off, on rising from our siesta,
for the Botanical Gardens. We enjoyed the journey
thither; we enjoyed exploring the Gardens and not-
ing the growth of things from week to week; we
enjoyed afternoon tea beside the lake; we enjoyed the
return journey; and, best of all, we tremendously
enjoyed each other's society. I endeavoured to keep
Thursday evenings free from engagements, so that I
could abandon myself to this delightful excursion
with a perfectly restful mind. It says something for
our Australian climate that only twice during those
thirteen years did the weather interfere with our
programme; and never once did we find it other
than pleasant, summer or winter, to take tea on the
open veranda of the kiosk.

We selected Thursday because I found it good to
make our weekly visit to the Botanical Gardens the
watershed of the week. Until then, I could give my
mind to any literary work I had on hand, allowing the
subjects for the coming Sunday to simmer in a remote
sub-consciousness. But, on returning from the Gardens,
my sermons occupied the entire foreground of my
thought and everything else was relegated to obscurity.

As soon as I had settled at Armadale, I applied for
membership in the Melbourne Cricket Club and,
after twelve years' waiting, obtained it. For some years
I had been President of the North Hobart Cricket Club
and, of course, a member of the Tasmanian Cricket
Association. Cricket has always occupied a large and
important place in my life. No member of the M.C.C.
is, I think, more regularly in his place than I am. The

game itself has been a sheer and unalloyed delight. The friendships forged at cricket have been among the most cherished and most valuable that I have known. And the sport has rendered me excellent service in one other way.

I have for years been troubled with insomnia, or, at least, with a persistent and obstinate sleeplessness. Many people, similarly plagued, have advised me to count sheep or to recite to myself texts of Scripture or passages of poetry. I have tried both schemes, hundreds of times, without avail. Giving them up as a bad job, I resort to cricket. There is something about cricket— I do not know what it is—that peculiarly impresses the memory. As beneath a magic wand, the incidents of cricket, with all their wealth of surrounding detail, are easily reconstructed in the mind. They come of their own accord, with no such mental effort as is required in the counting of sheep or the repetition of Scripture. And so, lying awake in the darkness, I see once more the green and shapely oval, fanned by the balmy breath of summer and fragrant with the peculiar but pleasant odour of the turf. I follow again the movements of the familiar figures in their creamy flannels. I revive those joyous moments that I have spent in concentration on the fluctuations and fortunes of the game. And thus, as long as I remain awake, I remain awake pleasantly, and, in the process, generate a mental atmosphere in which it is easy to fall asleep.

In 1926 a singular thing happened. I had been pondering deeply my College dream—three pastorates and then a few years of international and inter-denominational ministry. I was fifty-five and had been ten years at my third church. I was anxious to be still at my best when I set out upon the final phase: I dreaded lest the leaves of my life should be too deeply suffused with russet and saffron and bronze. And I was specially anxious to lay down my Armadale charge, and to hand it over to my successor whilst every department of the congregational activities was at high-water mark. I therefore decided to resign. A social evening was approaching. I made up my mind that, without hurling a bombshell among the teacups, I would, at that function, drop a clear hint of my intention. No statesman upon whose utterance the fate of nations depended ever weighed his words more carefully than I weighed the terms in which I proposed to make that discreet intimation. The evening arrived. Everything went splendidly. Towards the end of the programme a young lady sang a solo. As soon as she resumed her seat, I would speak my piece! My heart was in my mouth; I trembled in every limb. I was never more nervous in my life. The solo reached its close, and, under cover of the applause, the Secretary of the church, Mr. F. F. Lewis, mounted the platform. I was bewildered. What new development was this? As soon as silence was restored, he asked my wife and myself to approach him. He then paid a dainty little tribute to our ten years at Armadale, and, on behalf of the congregation, presented us each with a gold watch! I was never so taken aback in my life. Although I had learned to regard him as one of the best men breathing, I could have thrown the watches at him. My carefully prepared little speech was in fragments. My programme was smashed to smithereens! But I realized, almost instantly, that my plan had been a piece of my own architecture; the new development was obviously an expression of the will of God. And so we once more settled down to work and only relinquished the charge two years later under the pressure of circumstances that rendered our course unmistakable. And, even then, the leave-taking lacked that sense of finality which had added poignancy to our departures from Mosgiel and Hobart. For we knew that our new home would be within a mile or two of the church, and on two subsequent occasions, when Armadale has been without a minister, it has been my privilege to resume for a few months my old pulpit and minister afresh to my former congregation.

CHAPTER 27

GIPSYING

EARLY in 1927 I received a letter from Dr. F. A. Robinson of Toronto, inviting me to undertake a preaching tour throughout Canada and the United States in 1928. Dr. Robinson had organized the visits to those countries of Dr. F. B. Meyer, Dr. Campbell Morgan and Dr. Norwood. The idea of making so attractive a tour under such excellent auspices strongly appealed to me: it seemed an ideal realization of my college dream.

My only regret—a regret that I shall carry to my grave—is that, when the moment came for the superb adventure, I was totally unfit for the strain that it involved. A few weeks before sailing, I had the misfortune, through an accident in the city, to smash my hip. The shock affected my nerves; and, as a consecence, I was very much of an invalid when the day of embarkation came.

Notwithstanding this serious drawback, however, the tour was a most delightful and memorable experience. The lands that we now set out to visit offered us entirely new ground. One of the advantages of living in Australia, and of making periodical visits to the Homeland is that, since the distance from one extremity of the globe to the other is pretty much the same, whichever way you go, a man may, by varying his route, see most of the world in the process. We had made the long journey by way of Cape Horn, calling at Montevideo and Santa Cruz; we had several times rounded the Cape of Good Hope; and, on two or three occasions, we had travelled by way of Ceylon, Bombay, Aden, Suez, Port Said, Marseilles and Gibraltar. But the United States and Canada represented a field of novelty and romance.

We approached America by way of England, and, whilst in the Homeland, I fulfilled a heavy programme of engagements, including the preaching of the Missionary Sermon at the Baptist Union Assembly at Bristol. The opportunity of preaching this sermon was particularly welcome. All through my ministry, foreign missions have been the dearest passion of my heart. My rejection by the China Inland Mission only deepened my anxiety to serve the great cause on the home base. For nearly forty years I was honoured with seats on Missionary Committees, and in Victoria, for twelve years, I was Chairman. I like to think that my one public utterance in connexion with the Baptist Union of Great Britain was a plea for the evangelization of the world.

On our Canadian tour we sailed from Liverpool by the *Montclare* on July 7, landing at Montreal on the following Saturday evening. My first astonishment lay in being addressed as 'Doctor'. On our arrival in England in April, I found awaiting me a very kind letter from the Chancellor of McMaster University, inviting me to attend a ceremony of investiture at Toronto in June and to receive the degree of Doctor of Divinity.

I reflected that the McMaster hood had graced the shoulders of men like F. B. Meyer, Charles Brown, J. H. Shakespeare, J. H. Rushbrooke, and J. W. Ewing, that it had recently been conferred on W. Y. Fullerton, and that it was proposed that I should receive it simultaneously with G. W. Truett. I felt that such an honour was almost overpowering; yet acceptance seemed out of the question. My British engagements made it impossible for me to be in Toronto in June: the letter from the Chancellor contained no hint that the acceptance of the degree could be separated from personal attendance at the investiture; so, without saying a word to my parents, in whose home I was staying, or even to my wife, I penned and posted a grateful declinature.

On the following day I casually mentioned the matter. To my surprise, my father took it terribly to heart. He reminded me that he and my mother were getting very old; he said that they had always hoped, before they died, to see me wearing some such decoration; and he pleaded with me to send a cable reversing or modifying my previous decision. Grieved as I was to see them manifesting such disappointment, I felt that there was nothing to be done. On arrival at Montreal, however, I learned that the degree had been conferred *in absentia*. At that very moment a telegraph boy came along the deck. I hastily scribbled a cablegram to my parents and I learned afterwards that they were rudely awakened in the grey dawn of the following morning by the receipt of the message over the phone!

During the next few months we explored Canada

more thoroughly than we have ever explored any other country. I enjoyed the privilege of conducting services in every important centre, from Prince Edward Island and Nova Scotia in the east to Vancouver and Victoria on the Pacific seaboard. And, crossing the border many times, we visited the principal cities of the United States. Everywhere we were impressed by the charming hospitality so lavishly and eagerly extended to us; by the evident and sincere attachment of the people to their churches; and by their anxiety to learn all that we could impart concerning the conditions of life in the lands from which we came.

The southern states particularly intrigued us and there we were most touched by the thoughtfulness of the people. I should be ashamed of myself if, writing in this intimate way, I failed to place on record a couple of instances. The one occurred at Hollister in Missouri; the other at Montreat, North Carolina. At each of these places—as at many others—conferences were being held at which I was the guest speaker. With us, a conference suggests resolutions and amendments; but, in America, a conference is a gathering of hundreds or thousands of people, amidst the most enchanting scenery, for purely devotional purposes. I have never met with anything more inspiring or delightful. I would have given anything if the state of my health would have permitted my enjoying these opportunities of intercourse and fellowship to the full.

We were in the southern states in August; the heat was terrific; and I found the conditions exceedingly trying. My wife comforted me with the assurance that, in my public appearances, I gave no faintest indication of my exhaustion; but the strain was there; and I lost, first, my appetite and then my sleep.

The matron of the Missouri Conference, Mrs. Harriet F. Johnson, noticed that food no longer attracted me, and, in her kindly solicitude, broached my wife on the matter.

'I'm afraid that nothing can be done,' my wife replied. 'You see, your dishes are so different from those to which we are accustomed. Half the time we do not know what we are eating. If my husband were in health, he would revel in the novelty of it all. It seems too bad, because you are all so wonderfully kind; but there is nothing for it: we must hope and pray that his strength may hold out until we can get the dishes with which we are more familiar!' The matron went sadly away, but, in an hour's time, returned in evident glee.

'We have overcome your difficulty,' she exclaimed, excitedly. 'Away in the woods there,' she continued, taking my wife to the window, 'you can just see a pretty little bungalow: it is replete with every convenience: you are to live together there for the remainder of your stay. You can come to the hotel kitchen every day, and take the meat or poultry or fish that you fancy, and we will give you a maid to cook it in your own way, or, if you prefer it, you can cook it yourself. And you'll be away from all the rush and the bustle. When you feel like talking to the people, you can come across to the conference grounds; and when you feel like resting, you can rest!' This is the first of my two stories and the other resembles it.

At Montreat we were tremendously in love with everything and everybody. I revelled in the opportunity of pouring out my heart twice a day to thousands of people on the themes dearest to me. My health was better than at Missouri; but there was one thing for which we longed night and day. We Australians are inveterate tea-drinkers: we like tea often and we like it strong. But tea is simply unknown in the States and especially in the southern states. Coffee is king. The weird concoctions that were served up to us as tea were enough to make an Australian's blood run cold. We bravely struggled to conceal our ineffable disgust, but evidently our histrionic powers were unequal to the strain. And thus it came to pass that when, one afternoon, we returned to our room in the magnificent conference hotel at Montreat, we found on an occasional table a spirit lamp, a supply of tea, sugar and cream and all the requisites for helping ourselves! And when the time came to take a sad farewell of Carolina these gracious souls insisted on our packing up the entire box of tricks and taking it with us. How often we blessed them for their kindly—and therefore characteristic—thought. Even after the days of its usefulness were done, we preserved the spirit lamp as an eloquent monument to the American genius for imaginative hospitality.

I loved the eagerness of my American audiences to applaud a joke at their own expense. We often arrived at a place a few minutes before my first public appearance. My wife's would be the only familiar face to comfort me and I could not always find hers. It is not easy to become *en rapport* with one's hearers under such conditions. But, so situated, I invariably began with something like this:

'I come from Australia, and, to us Australians, you Americans seem strange people. Not that you *are* strange; but you *look* queer to us. For Australia, as you know, is a topsy-turvy kind of place. It is a place where we walk with our feet to your feet: a place whose midnight corresponds with your noon and whose noon corresponds with your midnight: a place where we get up when you go to bed and go to bed when you get up: a place where we celebrate Christmas at midsummer and keep the fourth of July in the depth of winter: a place where we go north in winter if we want to be warm and go south in summer if we want to be cool: a place where the trees shed their bark instead of their leaves, where the birds laugh and where all the native animals are fitted out with pockets. Now, just as all the world looks upside down to a man who is standing on his head, it is natural that, to us Australians, you Americans should appear odd. Here, in my hand, for example, is the programme of this gathering. The word *Program* is spelt with only seven letters. I am filled with admiration. The final letters of the word as we spell it are, of course, superfluous. But we British people never noticed that; and, if we had noticed it, we should have been too conservative to make the change. But you Americans both see and act. The thing that puzzles me, however, looking at things from our topsy-turvy Australian viewpoint, is that you, being such misers with your letters, are such spend-thrifts with your syllables. You cut the final letters out of program: you delete the *u* from color and honor and valor: you even paint the words GO SLO in enormous letters across your city streets: yet you call a lift an elevator, a car an automobile, a jug a pitcher, a tram a street-car, and so on. Now, this does strike us as peculiar. It would not be so bad if your long words were the right words and our short words

the wrong words. But our short words are the right words
and your long words are the wrong words. A lift is a lift:
it is not an elevator. You can lift a man up and lift him
down: but you can't elevate him up and elevate him
down. . . .'

And so on. By this time I had brought my audience
to a state of mind in which they would tolerate anything and my own enjoyment was unbounded.

This banquet of banter often served me in good
stead. We arrived one evening at a great southern
university. I soon discovered, to my horror, that,
through some absurd mistake, I had been advertised
to lecture on American Politics.

'I don't know a single thing about American Politics,'
I protested to the Chancellor and the Faculty as we
sat at dinner, 'and, even if I did, I would not lecture
on the subject: it isn't my line!'

My desperation was treated as a glorious jest. The
Chancellor assured me, with a beatific smile, that lots
of things would rush to my mind when I found myself
on my feet, and, an hour later, with all the assurance
in the world, he introduced me to an audience of two
or three thousand people. I was never in such straits.
I began with the passage that I have just cited and had
the satisfaction of seeing them laughing boisterously at
their own peculiarities. Then I switched over to an
address that I had been delivering all over the country
and that had no more to do with American Politics
than it had to do with the rings of Saturn. But, as a
concession to the proprieties, I solemnly remarked,
every now and again, that the application of this
principle to American politics was so obvious that it

would be an insult to the intelligence of a university audience if I were to labour the point. I closed with a reference to the warm friendship subsisting between America and Australia and resumed my seat amidst a thunder of applause. And to-day I prize among my choicest possessions a scroll bearing the seal of the university and the signature of its Chancellor assuring me that I delivered that night the most eloquent exposition of American Politics to which my learned audience had ever listened!

No audiences in the United States appealed to my heart more grippingly than these magnificent assemblies of students. I remember a Sunday night on which, after addressing an immense gathering at the University of Illinois, we were invited to take supper with the Chancellor and Faculty.

'In your travels through our country,' inquired the Chancellor, 'what has most impressed you?' I fancy that he expected me to reply that we had been most impressed by the wonders of Niagara Falls or by the splendours of the Rocky Mountains or by our drives across the prairies. All these had certainly thrilled us, but I could not give them pride of place.

'I can think of nothing,' I declared, 'that has moved me more deeply than the spectacle that I have just witnessed.' He pressed me for an explanation.

'I assure you,' I replied, 'that it stirred me to the very depths of my being to confront that vast array of students and to have the opportunity of pouring into their ears, for a solid hour, all that was best in my own heart.'

At other Universities, at the conferences and on many

such occasions, I was swept by a similar gust of emotion. The whole tour was a luxurious revelry: a noble feast of beautiful fellowship. I would give my right hand to repeat the experience, as I have several times been invited to do. But alas! I lack the physical strength that is essential, and must therefore content myself with a mingled diet of sweet memories and bitter regrets.

Chapter 28

ADIEU!

It is difficult to approach the final chapter of my life-story without contrasting the conditions under which I am closing my ministry with the conditions under which I opened it. In those primitive days, nobody dreamed of aeroplanes or of wireless sets. Telephones were novelties. The cinema was yet unborn. If my good people at Mosgiel wanted an evening's excitement, they organized a concert or a soirée.

And think of the change in methods of transportation! Those midnight drives across the Taieri Plain rush back upon me like a nightmare. Often, after a service or a meeting, I would climb into the seat of a buggy or a jinker, and, exposed to all kinds of weather, would drive for hours along roads that were a quagmire of slush and mud. Unable to see the deep ditches on either side, I had to trust to the goodness of God and the instinct of my horse. To-day a comfortable car, purring along excellent roads, would cover in twenty minutes a distance that then took me a couple of hours. Many a time, in visiting outlying districts, I have driven all day with the fluid mud swishing and oozing and swirling above the axle of my buggy watching the poor horse paddling bravely through the interminable swamp. Those were the good old days!

But let me resume the thread of my story! As, in

the course of our American tour, we made our way westward, with a view to returning by way of the Pacific, I began to realize that I was facing an enormous blank. From a life of ceaseless activity, I was going back to—nothing! I had resigned my church in order that I might exercise a peripatetic and inter-denominational ministry; but supposing nobody wanted such a ministry! Suppose no invitations came! The thought began to appal me. However, as we were sitting in the lounge of our hotel at Winnipeg, a bell-boy approached with a cablegram. Would I occupy for six months the pulpit of the Methodist Central Mission in Melbourne? I felt that this would represent an ideal inauguration of the kind of ministry I desired to exercise, and, with a heart overflowing with gratitude and delight, I cabled my acceptance.

From the hour at which, by way of Honolulu, Fiji and New Zealand, we returned to Melbourne, I have had few idle moments. Before my six months at the Methodist Central Mission had come to an end, the Rev. T. E. Ruth, of Pitt Street Congregational Church, Sydney, invited me to occupy his pulpit for six months whilst he visited the Homeland.

And so we spent a winter in Sydney. The whole experience was a distinctive and notable one. My ministry at Pitt Street—a grand old church in the very heart of the city—was one of the richest and most prosperous that I have known. And many things conspired to make our sojourn memorable. Incidentally, it was during those months that the immense and graceful arch that now spans the harbour, and that has taken its place as one of the wonders of the world, was constructed. Seeing that we were living at Manly, and crossing the water on the ferry several times a day, we enjoyed ample opportunity of entering into the wonder of this miracle of engineering. Millions of people now gaze upon the Sydney Bridge, and marvel at the magnitude of that miracle of engineering. But they can never experience in contemplating it the thrill that came to me. It was my good fortune to spend in Sydney the winter that marked the construction of that majestic arch. Day by day I watched it grow. As the two halves jutted out towards each other, we all wondered. Supposing that, in the alignment of one of those sections, the most infinitesimal error has been made! Suppose that, when they meet, one half is a yard higher than the other, or a yard to the west of the other! But, at last, in mid-air, they met and dovetailed perfectly! All Sydney held its breath for a moment in excited admiration and then a hundred sirens led the demonstration of triumphant delight.

Then, too, Australia tasted that winter the unprecedented novelty of listening-in at dead of night to the description of the Test Matches that were being played at Lords, the Oval, Old Trafford and other English grounds. Prominent among my recollections of those months in New South Wales is the weird memory of prowling about the house in the wee sma' hoors to ascertain Grimmett's latest victims and Bradman's latest score. And there were other adventures scarcely less captivating, including one that, whenever we recall it, occasions a singular medley of amusement and satisfaction.

On a very wet day we decided to slip across to the

city on the ferry, have lunch and return immediately.
As we were enjoying our soup at the café, however,
we became aware that the rain had entirely ceased;
and, by the time that we had finished our coffee, the
sun was shining brilliantly.

'Dear me,' I exclaimed, 'this is extraordinary! And
we have made no plans for the afternoon! We can't
go back and sit in the house on such a lovely day! I
wonder what we ought to do! We'll ask the waitress
to advise us!' At that very moment she arrived with
the ticket and I propounded our problem.

'We are strangers in Sydney,' I said, 'and we want
to make the best use of our time. Thinking that the
rain had set in for the day, we made no arrangements
for an outing this afternoon, but now that it has cleared
up so beautifully, we should like to take an excursion of
some sort. We had better select a trip by tram or by
ferry, so that we shall be in shelter if the rain returns.
Now what would you advise?' I saw before I had
finished speaking that my innocent question had
embarrassed her.

'I'm sorry,' she faltered, 'but I don't know anything
at all about it; I'll ask the other girls!'

'Oh,' I exclaimed, fancying that we had forged a
bond of sympathy and kinship, 'so you, too, are away
from home!'

'No,' she smiled, a trifle sadly, 'I was born here and
have slept in the same house every night since.'

'Well, then,' I replied, 'you must know all these
places, the names of which we see on the trams and
on the Quay—Coogee, Bondi, Clovelly, Bronte, La
Perouse, Fig Tree, Watson's Bay, and the rest. We

merely wanted you to suggest the best one to take in the circumstances.'

But it was of no use. All that she would say was that she would consult her companions, and, vanishing, she reappeared in company with another attractive apparition in blue and white, who quickly vouchsafed the guidance that we craved. Acting upon it, we spent a delightful afternoon on the Lane Cove River; but, again and again, our thoughts reverted to the girl at the restaurant and we resolved to attempt a solution of the mystery. This accounts for our presence at the corner table a few days later.

'I suppose you'll think it strange,' she said, 'but I've never been any of these trips. I was born at Balmoral, just across the harbour, and I live there still. I come over on the ferry every day to work and go back again every night. And that's all the travelling I've ever done. I've never been on a train or a steamer, or anything like that. I've only once been into the city and that was a long time ago. I've never been to a church or a concert or a theatre or a picture show. I hear the other girls talking of the places that they go to at nights and during the weekends; but, somehow, I have no desire to see these things for myself. I was brought up to live a stay-at-home kind of life; and now it has become a fixed habit; and I don't want to go anywhere or see anything.'

My wife reasoned with her, urging her to break her hermit habit, and we came away. A month or two later, however, we returned and found our little waitress inordinately excited by our reappearance.

'I don't know how to tell you,' she exclaimed; 'it

all seems too lovely; and it began that day when you were last here. After the midday rush was over, some of us—one or two of the cooks and a few of the girls —were standing talking in the kitchen; and, just in fun, I told them that you had been giving me a terrible dressing-down. Charlie Jackson, one of the boys that work here, said that it served me right. Charlie's a nice boy; I always liked him; and I knew he didn't mean to be nasty. He came to me afterwards and said that, on the following Sunday, he was going for a run on his motor-bike through the Hawkesbury River district; he asked me to go with him, either in the side-car or riding pillion. I went,' she exclaimed, clasping her hands ecstatically, 'and oh, it was beautiful. Beautiful! And,' she added, 'we've had several trips together since then!' And not long afterwards they were married.

During that winter we visited all the prisons and penal establishments of New South Wales, we inspected all the halls, homes and institutions of the City Mission, and we were the guests, during one memorable evening, of the officers of the Salvation Army. I was deeply moved when Mrs. Carpenter, the wife of General Carpenter, herself the biographer of so many eminent Salvationists, told me that Commissioner Howard, old General Booth's right-hand man during the early days of the Army, died clasping my *Bunch of Everlastings* in his hand.

I had to thank the officers of the Army for advice that was invaluable to me in dealing with cases of a kind with which I had never been brought into contact before. In the course of my life and ministry I have witnessed many astounding triumphs of redeeming grace. I could very easily write a book that would augment the literature of striking conversions and incredible transformations. But I never had to do with cases more dramatic or more affecting than those that passed through my hands in the course of that memorable winter. I shall always feel grateful to Mr. Ruth for the door of opportunity that he then threw open to me.

In 1931, the year following our visit to Sydney, I appreciated the privilege of delivering, in Adelaide, the Bevan Lectures on Preaching. It was in Adelaide that I spent a memorable hour with old Sir Langdon Bonython who told me that he distinctly remembered, as a little boy, sitting on the knee of his grandmother in Cornwall whilst she told him how, as a little girl, *she* had perched upon the knee of Mr. John Wesley during one of his visits to her parents' home. I thought this one of the most interesting links with the past that I, personally, had ever met. In the same year, I was invited to minister, for a month or two, at Albert Street Church in Brisbane—the central Methodist pulpit in that delightful city. This led to our returning, the following year, not only for a second ministry in Brisbane, but for a comprehensive tour of the immensities of Queensland, including the tropical north and the Great Barrier Reef. It was a most romantic and adventurous journey, covering some thousands of miles, through the most picturesque landscapes that Australia possesses. To stay at sugar plantations, cattle stations, out-back farms and in the mining areas represented a continuous romance, whilst the colourful landscapes that presented themselves like an ever-changing panorama rendered it almost incredible that we were still in our own familiar Australia. Every creek and lagoon is adorned with the most beautiful water-lilies, pink and white and blue and gold. For mile after mile, as we surveyed the country from the railway train, the immediate foreground twinkled with acres of heliotrope ageratum, pink cosmos, sky blue convolvulus and crimson lantana. Very frequently the tinted grasses, catching the sunlight, blazed like a blood-red sea. Amidst the verdure of the evergreen bush, Nature allows the foliage to assume seasonal patches of saffron, crimson and gold, whilst the scarlet flame-tree and the wine-coloured eugenias contribute their flaunting splashes of brightness. Everywhere birds of gleaming plumage—especially the cockatoos, the parrots and the kingfishers—add gay pigments to the panorama, whilst the papilio butterflies—as big as birds and as blue as delphiniums or cornflowers—flutter to and fro in every leafy valley. If you turn to the seaside, you find the waters flashing with the kaleidoscopic shades of the rainbow-tinted coral. And, as though this lavish colour-scheme were not sufficiently generous, the very sunsets of the north are distinctly more gorgeous than those to be seen elsewhere, the fiery hues softening, as they fade, into infinite gradations of delicate tinting.

One incident connected with this tropical journey is likely to haunt our memories until our last sun sets. We were driving in the neighbourhood of Lake Barrine, a deep, blue pool that nestles shyly and silently amidst a dense belt of evergreen jungle. A cassowary, emerging from the forest, stood for a moment defying the advance of our car. As soon as it had resumed its progress and vanished into the bush, we met a man who told us that he had just passed a python asleep in the undergrowth. Aflame with curiosity, we set out in search of it. It was not hard to find. Its fifteen feet of reptilian ugliness glistened in the sparkling sunshine. It was lost in the profoundest slumber—the long sleep that should have ended only with the spring. An exhibit in a museum could not have seemed more remote from life. In hope of seeing some faint squirm or twitch, we tickled it and prodded it; but all to no purpose. Then, seizing a stouter branch, we essayed to lever up its head to get a better look at it. But we had carried our senseless liberties too far. The horrid creature woke up, not gradually, but suddenly, and turned savagely upon us. We scurried to the car as quickly as our legs would carry us, and when, on gaining that welcome retreat, we slammed the door behind us, the reptile already had his head upon the running-board. For many nights after this adventure, we awoke in a cold perspiration, living once more through those tense and terrifying seconds and steadfastly resolving, in future, to let sleeping dogs—and other things—lie!

It was often difficult to realize that our visit to these latitudes was being paid in winter-time. One Sunday morning I was lounging in coat sleeves on a deck-chair on the veranda of the parsonage, glancing over the notes of the sermon that, in an hour's time, I should be preaching. Men in silk suits, and women with bare arms and in flimsiest frocks, were moving up and down the streets, whilst, in most of the living-rooms, electric fans were in motion. My wife suddenly approached me, and I fear that my mind was more intently focused upon my sermon notes than upon her remarks.

'Do you notice,' she asked, 'how they build their houses up here—every room opening into other rooms and every room opening on to the veranda?'

'Oh, yes,' I replied, absently, 'it's all very well at this time of year, but it must be precious cold in winter!' And it was winter—actual mid-winter—at the time!

In ministries of this kind, some near at hand and some far afield, twelve happy years have been spent. The only element of permanence and continuity has been represented by my Wednesday lunch-hour service at Scots Church—the central Presbyterian Church in the city of Melbourne. Three years ago the Session of Scots Church graciously invited me to conduct this service as a gesture of helpfulness to the business men and women of the city. It has been to me a constant and growing delight. The vision of these men and women from shops and offices and banks, hungry for some spiritual refreshment in the middle of the day, has moved me to the depths of my being and has called out all that is best in me. It has been an excellent discipline for me, in days in which I was tempted to repeat incessantly the same sermons and addresses, to be under the necessity of preparing at least one new utterance every week. And it seemed positively providential that, at the very moment at which my doctor advised me to submit myself no longer to the strain of week-night engagements, this opportunity should present itself of pouring out my soul, once each week, without disturbing the repose of my evenings. God is wonderfully good, and I have felt extremely grateful to Him, as well as to the minister and officers of Scots Church, for opening to me this door of happy service.

During these twelve years I have preached an almost exactly equal number of times in the pulpits of the various denominations and have felt equally at home in each. Indeed, I have liked to think of myself as a kind of shuttle, moving to and fro between the churches, and, perhaps, binding them a little closer together. And it does seem to me that, if one man can move among all the denominations, preaching the same sermons everywhere with equal acceptance, the differences between the churches must be very much less vital than we sometimes think.

The whole experience has been wonderfully enjoyable. The fellowship with ministers, officers and congregations of all denominations has been, literally, too beautiful for words.

In 1936 we once more visited the Homeland, and were again touched by the warmth of the welcome accorded us. As we review lives that are now growing fairly long and in the course of which we have many times girdled the globe and seen most of its peoples, we are touched to tears by the beautiful memory of all those choice and charming spirits who, on every shore, have extended hands of the most bounteous hospitality and have won our hearts by their sheer and simple goodness. How little I dreamed when, as a student, I set out on my lonely voyage to the uttermost ends of the earth, that I should one day find myself occupying the historic pulpits—Wesley's, Spurgeon's, Parker's, and the rest—in which, in youth, I had heard the giants of a bygone day! I never stepped upon the platforms of the great May meetings—and I spoke in the Queen's Hall three times in one day—without pinching myself to make sure that I was not dreaming. In the course of that tour I had the unique experience of preaching—often several times—in every county in England.

One thing I should like to record in connexion with these gipsyings. During the thirty-four years that I spent in my three pastorates, I very seldom had the satisfaction of saying to myself on Sunday night: 'I have led a man to Christ to-day!' From this point of view I looked back upon my ministry with heavy discontent: it had seemed woefully fruitless and ineffective. Yet, during the years of travel, we constantly encountered men and women who came long distances to meet me in order that they might tell me of some sermon, preached at Mosgiel or Hobart or Armadale, by which they had been led into Christian life and service. Let other ministers, taking note, repine no more!

Two experiences that had never before been mine made the 1936 tour memorable. I was invited to address the General Assembly of the Church of Scotland at Edinburgh. The Moderator, Professor Daniel Lamont, D.D., was kind enough to introduce me as 'the man whose name is on all our lips, whose books are on all our shelves, and whose illustrations are in all our sermons.' I spoke for three-quarters of an hour on Modern Evangelism, and, with such a theme and such an audience, enjoyed myself immensely. At the close of my address, the Moderator most graciously invited me to sit beside him on the dais for the rest of the evening. A day or two later I was entertained at a public breakfast in the city of Edinburgh. Lord Wark presided and, with Bailie John T. Falconer, LL.B., W.S., on behalf of the city, Dr. Carstairs on behalf of the literary world, and a number of other distinguished speakers, said many all-too-generous things.

The other memorable experience was a most delightful visit to Ireland, a country we had never before seen. We approached the Emerald Isle by air, flying from Birmingham, and the panoramic view of the Isle of Man obtained in the course of that flight was one of the loveliest spectacles on which our eyes have rested. We looked forward to our Irish tour with almost childlike excitement; but the reality put every anticipation to shame. How can I forget the closing meeting of the series? It was held in the University Road Methodist Church, Belfast, which was crowded to the doors. After I had pronounced the benediction, a voice from the body of the church cried, 'Can't we see Mrs. Boreham?' The people resumed their seats and applauded vigorously. The Chairman, Dr. Marshall, asked Mrs. Boreham, if present, to come to the pulpit. I shall like, in my last hours, to recall the scene that followed. It was one of the proudest moments of my life. Escorted by Mr. J. Lynn Hazelton and Mr. Norman Robb, officers of the church, my wife made her way up the aisle amidst an overwhelming ovation. She happened to be attired in a costume that I thought the most becoming and attractive in her wardrobe. Mounting the pulpit, all grace and dignity and charm, she smiled and bowed her acknowledgements. I loved Ireland for loving her. No plaudits were ever more richly merited and certainly none ever fell more sweetly upon my own ears.

LAUS DEO!

My tale is told! I feebly tried
  God's loving-kindness to record;
And now I lay my pen aside
  With deep thanksgiving to my Lord.